STEPHANIE HIRSH AND JOELLEN KILLION

The Learning Educator

A New Era for Professional Learning

NATIONAL STAFF DEVELOPMENT COUNCIL

National Staff Development Council
5995 Fairfield Road, #4
Oxford, OH 45056
513-523-6029
800-727-7288
Fax: 513-523-0638
E-mail: NSDCoffice@nsdc.org
www.nsdc.org

The Learning Educator:
A New Era in Professional Learning
By Stephanie Hirsh and Joellen Killion
Editor: Joan Richardson
Copy editor: Bill Rapai
Designer: Sue Chevalier

Printed in the United States of America
Item #B372

ISBN: 978-0-9800393-0-6

TABLE OF CONTENTS

INTRODUCTION

I n the last decade, the field of staff development has undergone many changes. All of these changes, from our perspective, are good. We, too, have undergone tremendous changes in how we think about and practice staff development. We wish we could say that we had originated all of the ideas you will read about in this book. The truth, however, is that many people enlightened us. Their ideas, research, advocacy, and practices have shaped what we think about professional learning and what we propose for the next decade. Their names will appear repeatedly throughout this book. Chief among them is Dennis Sparks whose leadership of NSDC has influenced each of us significantly.

Some might say that the principles in this book are merely *Sparksisms*. We cannot avoid the deep influence he has had on our thinking about this field, nor do we wish to. We hope he is proud of the ideas. As

we move into the next decade, we want to focus our attention on implementation of these ideas. The speed of change is too slow and the failure to move more quickly impacts educators and students alike.

In shaping our ideas, we realize that we are a product of those whom we respect and who have been our teachers. We also listen to our critics as they question the importance of collaboration, developing teacher expertise, the balance between district-provided and school-centered professional learning, or the impact of professional learning on student learning. We draw strength from the criticisms we hear because we know this means the ideas are causing others to think about the importance of professional learning.

The hallmark of a great idea, in our minds, is one that will resonate with others. Some great ideas, in fact, ideas that have reshaped literally how we think about the world, were widely scoffed at. Think Newton and Copernicus! While these ideas have indeed changed the way we think, too much energy and time was spent on cultivating a widespread acceptance of the idea itself. Instead, we propose a set of principles that will sound familiar because we have been laying the groundwork for them for the last decade. When we speak publicly or write about professional learning, these ideas have been part of our message.

We are not as interested in acceptance of the ideas we propose as we are in the actions they generate. We are ready now to invest our energy in two things. First, we want to demonstrate that these ideas are legitimate. They are supported by research, both by the expert perspective of thought leaders in the field and by practitioners who can tell their own stories of success. To this end, we share the evidence to support the principles you will read about in this book. We want to end the debate about the value of professional development and its impact on leading, teaching, and learning, and move to action.

Second, we want to provide a consolidated resource that outlines what we expect to see in practice. We want each principle to be represented not in an occasional school or school system. We are ready to move these principles into action in all schools and all school systems. Too few educators have opportunities for professional learning that is a part of their daily work. As a result, too few educators are contributing to practices that improve student learning.

What we advocate now is simply this: We no longer feel compelled to justify the value or importance of professional learning. We want to focus our attention on professional learning that will create a culture of collective responsibility that gets results for students. Our principles strive to do this. Each principle describes professional learning in action. If professional development decision makers accept the principles, then their decisions and actions will contribute positively to ensure that professional learning will improve leading, teaching, and learning. If there is not consensus on the principle, subsequent actions and decisions may contribute to the fragmentation of professional development efforts and results.

Over the next decade, we plan to ensure that every educator engages in effective professional learning every day so every student learns. This book, we hope, helps readers understand what qualifies as effective professional learning, enables them to believe that this kind of professional learning is possible to achieve, and provides a blueprint that enables thought leaders, researchers, and practitioners to join together in this crucial work.

ACKNOWLEDGEMENTS

The preparation of this manuscript began as a challenge to look forward to the next decade. The journey was one of discovery, synthesis, and visioning. We challenged and clarified each other's thinking, gained insight and resolve, wrote and rewrote each other's words, found differences that strengthened the results of our collaborative work, and valued each other tremendously.

At each step, we realized that we were not alone in our work. In addition to each other, researchers, thought leaders, and countless practitioners influenced every step. We are especially grateful to educators in schools whose day-to-day work gives us the greatest hope that students will learn. We appreciate each one. Without their work, this book would not exist.

Two people in particular merit a special thank you. The first is Dennis Sparks, NSDC's emeritus executive director. For 23 years, he devoted himself to leading NSDC and shaping the field of professional learning. His influence on our thinking cannot be measured. Through his reading, writing, and dialoguing with us, he has helped us clarify our message about professional learning in the next decade.

The second is Hayes Mizell, NSDC's distinguished senior fellow. For the last decade, Hayes' voice has been our touchstone. He never wavers from his beliefs and principles and holds us and NSDC to a high standard of single-minded focus — professional development that impacts student learning. He has served as our critical friend and our supporter.

We are grateful to our NSDC colleagues, particularly to Joan Richardson, NSDC's director of communications, and her staff who so carefully prepared our manuscript for press. Joan's thoughtful attention as our editor to our every word brought clarity and precision to the text. While our attention was focused on the book, we were each supported by many around us who kept our offices and NSDC operating smoothly.

In the preparation of the manuscript, we had the special assistance of Patty Yoo, former assistant principal from Richardson Independent School District in Dallas, Texas, who served as our research assistant. She helped ensure that the references and citations are accurate.

Each of us has many people to thank for their support and guidance during the time we were writing this book.

Stephanie: In addition to Dennis Sparks and Hayes Mizell, I recognize the NSDC Board of Trustees past and present. Your willingness to commit your time and expertise to the Council's purpose has contributed significantly to my thinking and many of the examples we share. In addi-

tion, I thank the NSDC staff for incredible support during my tenure. Your leadership and practice embody daily many of the principles outlined in this text. I thank my family for its unwavering encouragement and support. Throughout my tenure with NSDC, my interactions with educators have helped me to clarify what is important in our work. I hope this books helps others to clarify what is essential and how to achieve the results they seek.

Joellen: I'm grateful for my husband, Terry, whose love, support, and warm office afforded me many hours of focused attention to this text. I'm thankful for my children, Sara and Greg, and my stepson, Jeff, who give me courage to take on challenging tasks. I am particularly appreciative for my 90-year-old father, Santo Palazzolo, who taught me anything is possible if one persists. He modeled this lesson each day of his life.

OVERVIEW

I n *A New Vision for Staff Development* (1997), Dennis Sparks and Stephanie Hirsh called for a paradigm shift in the way educators viewed staff development. The authors advanced a new form of staff development that was results-driven, standards-based, and job-embedded. These three phrases continue to be used to describe a powerful vision for high-quality professional learning that influences student learning. Combined with school-focused and content-rich, the phrases continue to paint a vision of the professional development we want for all educators. Perhaps no other words have replaced these since too few districts have successfully implemented this vision for high-quality professional learning.

Results-driven. We continue to advocate for results-driven professional development for individuals, teams, schools, systems, and states. Stephen Covey said,

"begin with the end in mind" (1989, p. 95). Results-driven staff development calls on educators to begin planning for professional development with the question: What do students need to know and be able to do? That leads to the question: What do educators need to know and be able to do to ensure students successfully meet their objectives? And concludes with, what professional development is necessary to support the development of knowledge and skills educators need to produce the desired results for students?

Standards-based. Staff development standards define the best practices associated with desired outcomes for staff development. Staff development standards guide planning, implementation, and assessment. They distinguish between effective and ineffective practices, and offer benchmarks for describing excellence. NSDC's Standards for Staff Development (2001) were developed by representatives of 20 leading education associations and involved a thorough review of the most current and relevant research linking staff development and student results. The standards have been adopted by more than half the states and many more have used NSDC's standards to develop their own standards.

NSDC's standards address content, process, and context issues. Content standards address the "what" question of professional learning. What knowledge and skills will educators acquire and how will they and their students benefit? "Not all content is created equal" reminds us of the importance of the content standards.

Process standards address the "how" question of professional learning. How do we design professional learning so that competency in new practices is accelerated for educators? "Training without follow-up is malpractice" reinforces the significance of the process standards.

Context standards address the organization's responsibility to build a climate and culture that is receptive to and supportive of new practices that develop its leaders, and provide the necessary resources to sustain improvement. Content, process, and context addressed simultaneously allow professional learning to produce its intended results.

Job-embedded. Job-embedded requires that most of an educator's professional learning occurs during the workday in the work place, is designed to support team learning, and is offered and available to all educators. Job-embedded means the learning occurs during the workday and has a direct link to the goals set for students by the team and the school. NSDC's oft-repeated phrase, "At school, everyone's job is to learn," captures the essence of job-embedded learning.

In 1997, Sparks and Hirsh described shifts that called for some changes in practice to occur more frequently than other practices (p. 12). They included:
- From individual development to individual development and organizational development;
- From fragmented, piecemeal improvement efforts to staff development driven by a clear, coherent strategic plan for the school district, each school, and the departments that serve schools;
- From district-focused to school-focused approaches to staff development;
- From a focus on adult needs and satisfaction to a focus on student needs and learning outcomes, and changes in on-the-job behaviors;
- From training conducted away from the job as the primary delivery system for staff development to multiple forms of job-embedded learning;
- From having "experts" transmit knowledge and skills to teachers to providing opportunities for teachers to study teaching and learning processes themselves;
- From a focus on generic instructional skills to a combination of generic and content specific skills;
- From staff developers who function primarily as trainers to those who provide consultation, planning, and facilitation services as well as training;
- From staff development provided by one or two departments to staff development as a critical function and major responsibility performed by all administrators and teacher leaders;
- From staff development directed toward teachers as the primary recipients to continuous improvement in performance for everyone who affects student learning; and

- From staff development as a frill that can be cut during difficult financial times to staff development as an indispensable process without which schools cannot hope to prepare young people for citizenship and productive employment (pp. 12-16).

While some districts have made a significant shift in how they approach professional development, too few districts have made the shift called for in 1997. We believe that:

- Pockets of innovation exist, but are not the norm;
- Quality instruction exists, although it is not consistently provided to all students and, in particular, students who need it most;
- Quality learning environments exist for some students, but are not pervasive; and
- Quality tools and resources exist to support staff development, but are not used comprehensively.

Few school systems and schools can document successful alignment of their staff development efforts with all the paradigm shifts.

Several events occurred in the last 10 years that also impacted how we think about and approach staff development. By far, the most influential has been the standards movement followed closely by the accountability movement. The expectation that students be held accountable for achieving standards and that schools be ranked according to the success of their students introduced a new phenomenon into education. Public celebrations as well as sanctions for students and later for school systems, schools, and finally individual educators put new pressure on the field.

Most students are being asked to do something that had been previously expected of only some students. All teachers are being asked to do something that was previously only asked of some teachers. Most teachers are neither prepared to help *all* students achieve high standards or teach the content that is now covered on high-stakes tests. An immediate response is to find "silver bullet" solutions: If teachers just work harder, if students have better incentives, if teachers teach the right curriculum, if, if, if all possible solutions are debated by the public, and a few get it right. School districts needed to reconsider how to help teachers help their students.

Not only is more expected of students, but expectations of teachers for student performance are higher and schools seek strategies for ensuring all students are more successful. Researchers and practitioners alike seek answers to challenges of students who previously were not successful. Research demonstrated that the quality of teaching is the single greatest determinant in the success of students. Ultimately, no silver bullet exists. Instead, educators realize what staff developers have known for a long time: Staff development is the most powerful intervention to ensure more students experience higher quality teaching every day.

More is expected of professional development, and educators are responding. While political agendas come and go, we suspect that the shifts we see and the others we predict for professional development will never return to the status quo of the end of the 20th century. Educators will continue to expect more from professional development because they have experienced more. As *A New Vision for Staff Development* guided the field for almost a decade, we hope that the fundamental principles offered in this volume will be a valuable foundation for staff development discussions for the next decade.

Knight (2007) wrote, "Human action is based on a theory or principles, and to fully understand what we stand for, we should think deeply about what principles we embrace for our work and personal lives" (p. 53). We offer our fundamental principles as the guideline for decisions and actions related to professional learning. We believe a set of guiding principles regarding professional learning is more important than predicting the future or providing a prescription for action. We hope that our principles coupled with those that you have developed in your own work will assist you in coming years as you work to ensure that all students achieve great results.

"The value of a good theory," says Knight, "is that it provides a way for people to organize, prioritize, and choose how they will act and what they will do in any situation, and, for that reason, a theory can be very practical" (2007, p. 38). Later, Knight says, "Theory is the gravity that holds together any systematic approach" (p. 39). We hope you view the principles we share as extremely practical and helpful as you confront many of the roadblocks to effective professional development.

REFERENCES

Covey, S. (1989). *The seven habits of highly effective people.* New York: Simon & Schuster.

Knight, J. (2007). *Instructional coaching: A partnership approach to improving instruction.* Thousand Oaks, CA: Corwin Press.

National Staff Development Council. (2001). *NSDC's standards for staff development (revised).* Oxford, OH: Author.

Sparks, D. & Hirsh, S. (1997). *A new vision for staff development.* Arlington, VA: ASCD and NSDC.

"Important principles may and must be inflexible."
— *Abraham Lincoln*

PRINCIPLES

Principles shape our thoughts, words, and actions.

P rinciples shape our thoughts, words, and actions. They influence our decisions. They guide us in problem solving. They serve as touchstones that we continually return to when we face conflict, dilemmas, or challenges. They set a common foundation shared by members of a community. Members of the community are also challenged to uphold and protect the principles because they shape what the community stands for.

Each person lives by a set of principles. Some of our principles are unquestioned and fundamental to who we are. Some are new to us and through our experiences and dialogue we continue to clarify and deepen our understanding of them. Our principles guide our work, thoughts, goals, actions, and decisions.

Principles are underlying assumptions required in a system of thought and are often spoken of as laws for moral or ethical decision making. We frequently hear, "It's the principle of it." The Oxford English Dictionary defines a principle in this way:

- "Origin, source; source of action; fountainhead.

- "A fundamental source from which something proceeds; a primary element, force, or law which produces or determines particular results; the ultimate basis upon which the existence of something depends; cause, in the widest sense.

- "A fundamental truth or proposition, on which many others depend; a primary truth comprehending, or forming the basis of, various subordinate truths; a general statement or tenet forming the (or a) ground of, or held to be essential to, a system of thought or belief; a fundamental assumption forming the basis of a chain of reasoning.

- "A general law or rule adopted or professed as a guide to action; a settled ground or basis of conduct or practice; a fundamental motive or reason of action, esp. one consciously recognized and followed" (OED).

The principles in this book intend to guide the thought, words, and actions of leaders of professional learning. Those leaders include both school and system leaders in formal and informal leadership roles. Leaders are those whose work influences the shape of professional learning in schools and school systems.

The eight principles in this book, listed at right, establish a foundation for professional learning.

Each statement is a proposition about professional learning. The authors offer these principles as their teachable points of view to guide decision making and actions related to professional learning, to serve as the foundation for the standards that define the success of professional learning, and to strengthen the results that educators hope to achieve through professional learning. A teachable point of view, according to Noel Tichy (2002), is "a cohesive set of ideas and concepts that a person is able to articulate to others" (p. 78). "A teachable point of view," says Sparks (2007), "reveals clarity of thought regarding ideas and values and is a tool that enables leaders to communicate those ideas and values to others" (p. 47).

Principles endure over time. They supersede time, programs, strategies, and current practices. They serve as the driver behind programs, strategies, and practice. Principles shape and drive what we say, think, and do. What we say, think, and do conversely serve as the symbolic indicators to others of our principles. Our words and actions convey how deeply we hold our principles. Our principles also can create dissonance within ourselves if we act and speak in a way that is incongruent with

THE PRINCIPLES

Principle 1: Principles
Principles shape our thoughts, words, and actions.

Principle 2: Diversity
Diversity strengthens an organization and improves its decisions.

Principle 3: Leadership
Leaders are responsible for building the capacity in individuals, teams, and organizations to be leaders and learners.

Principle 4: Planning
Ambitious goals lead to powerful actions and remarkable results.

Principle 5: Focus
Maintaining the focus of professional learning on teaching and student learning produces academic success.

Principle 6: Impact
Evaluation strengthens performance and results.

Principle 7: Expertise
Communities can solve even their most complex problems by tapping internal expertise.

Principle 8: Collaboration
Collaboration among educators builds shared responsibility and improves student learning.

them. They can be the source of deep conflict between people or the source of strong alliances among people.

In this book, we identify the principles

that we hope will shape practices in professional learning for the next decade and beyond. Rather than recommend specific practices for schools and districts to adopt or adapt, we identify the principles that will drive the professional learning. We offer principles rather than practices because they are the fountainhead from which specific practices emerge. We encourage schools and districts to create their own, contextually appropriate practice variations based on the foundation of these principles. When the principles serve as the foundation for decisions, variations in practice will have integrity. Practices are "what to do's," according to Covey, while principles are "why to do's" (p. 25). Principles shape those practices.

SUPPORTING EVIDENCE

"What separates a learning community from an ordinary school is its collective commitment to guiding principles that articulate what the people in the school believe and what they seek to create," states Pasi (2003). "Furthermore, these guiding principles are not just articulated by those in positions of leadership; even more important, they are embedded in the hearts and minds of people throughout the school" (p. 15).

Principles shape policy makers' and educators' decisions and actions related to professional development. When educators hold a common set of principles as the foundation for their practice, their actions are more aligned with goals and with each other. In *Good to Great* (2001), Collins recommends that businesses preserve a set of core values or principles while stimulating progress and change. "Enduring, great companies preserve their core values and purpose while their business strategies and operating practices endlessly adapt to a changing world. There is the magical combination of 'preserve the core and stimulate progress'" (p. 195). The core principles keep the company grounded even amid rapid changes.

Sometimes, efforts to find a quick fix or rapid change work against the laws of nature. It is unreasonable to expect overnight change in habits of mind and routines. Change of this type is a journey of experimentation that results in successes and failures. The laws of nature, the principles of change, tell us that deep change is more than doing something differently. Deep change or transformational learning, according to Dennis Sparks, is "changes in beliefs and assumptions that affect professional practice. Transformational learning is based on the view that an individual's beliefs influence his or her actions in powerful ways that may or may not be evident to the person. While an educator's belief system may be called by different names — mental model, paradigm, worldview — that belief system exerts considerable influence on teaching and leadership" (2003, p. 29). If the purpose of professional learning is to refine and improve professional practice and produce results for students, then we must evaluate professional learning by both how it changes practice and how it impacts student learning. Gains in professional practice without concomitant gains in student learning are not what we desire.

Covey explores the role of principles in leadership and personal change in his book, *Principle-Centered Leadership* (1991). He suggests that when we think about change, even if the desire for change is generated from within, "we usually think in terms of learning new skills rather than showing more integrity to basic principles. But significant breakthroughs often represent internal breaks with traditional ways of thinking" (pp. 17-18). When our actions, leadership, lives, and relationships are centered on "true north" principles, according to Covey, we are more effective. "Our effectiveness is predicated upon certain inviolate principles — natural laws in the human dimension that are just as real, just as unchanging, as laws such as gravity are in the physical dimension" (p. 18).

We do not invent principles; they exist in nature in arenas other than in education. We bring them into the limelight for examination, elaboration, and expansion. We bring them to the forefront so they can be shared with and explored by others. Principles exist in both personal and professional practice equally, in human relationships and in organization. We focus on the principles of professional learning. "To the degree people recognize and live in harmony with such basic principles as fairness, equity, justice, integrity, honesty, and trust," says Covey, "they move toward either survival and stability on the one hand or disintegration and destruction on the other (1991, p. 18).

Principles are like compasses, Covey says. "They are always pointing the way" (1991, p. 19). They act like the sun and North Star in celestial navigation. They help define a course toward the destination or set the lost sailor back on course. When challenges arise, principles help ease the struggle and find the course. They remain unchanged regardless of the environment. Principles become habits of mind and behavior "enabling fundamental transformations of individuals, relationships, and organizations" (p. 19).

Schon (1983), Argyris (1982), and Senge (1990) describe personal principles as the beliefs people hold or their mental model. A mental model is a set of "images, assumptions, and stories that we carry in our minds of ourselves, other people,

institutions, and every aspect of the world" (Senge, Roberts, Ross, Smith, & Kleiner, 1994). Schon describes two types of mental models that shape what people think and how they act. One kind of mental model is espoused theories [principles], those that people profess. Yet sometimes contradicting espoused theories [principles] are theories-in-use [principles-in-action]. Wheatley (2003) acknowledges that, "as humans, we often contradict ourselves. We say one thing and do another. We state who we are, but then act contrary to that. We say we're open-minded, but then judge someone for their appearance. We say we're a team, but then gossip about a colleague" (p.18).

Theories, according to Knight (2007), are principles that explain how things work. As stated in the Overview, a good theory "provides a way for people to organize, prioritize, and choose how they will act and what they will do in any situation, and for that reason a theory can be very practical" (p. 38).

Principles-in-use are manifested in a person's behaviors and words. They fundamentally shape what a person says, thinks, or does. When a principal says she supports parental involvement in her school (espoused principle) and yet creates a complicated system for registering parent volunteers who come into the school (principle-in-action), her espoused principle and her principle-in-action contradict one another. Seeing this contradiction may be difficult for her but relatively easy for others to recognize. "Some of these implicit beliefs unknowingly impede progress toward our goals," suggests Sparks (2007). "A part of us — our intentions — wants to go in one direction. Another part of us — our beliefs — may act as a brake that slows our progress" (p. 62).

In the 1950s, two University of

THE JOHARI WINDOW

Other	Known to others and not to me	Not known to others or to me
	Known to others and to me	Known to me and not to others
	Self	

California researchers who were studying personalities created the Johari Window to help explain how it is possible for us to have contradictory mental models (Luft, 1969). (The name of the diagram comes from the combination of creators' two names, Joe Luft and Harry Ingham.) The Johari Window is a diagram that portrays two people looking at a house from two different perspectives. Inside the house are four rooms. From one side, an individual can see only two of the four rooms. From the other side, an individual can see one room seen by the other person and also one room that the other person does not see. Two rooms from any perspective remain hidden.

The application of the Johari Window, according to its creators, is in opening and expanding the public area, the area of information known to others and to self and minimizing the private areas — those areas known to one and not the other or to neither. This can best be done, they say, by honest feedback, exchange of information, and dialogue about principles in action. If a person acts in a way that is not consistent with his or her espoused principles, honest, constructive feedback helps the person open up what is not known by placing that information into the "known to self and others" area.

The principal we described earlier is unable to recognize that her behaviors discouraged rather than encouraged parental involvement in school. Yet parents and even staff may recognize this. They see what the principal is unable to see. When they describe behaviors to her, they can identify what makes parents feel unwelcome. By offering that to the principal in open, honest communication, the principal becomes aware of her belief-in-action, moving it from the private area to her public area. And, if she wants to exhibit the belief that parents are welcome in the school, she can adjust what she says, does, and thinks so that they are congruent with her espoused belief.

Every person and organization has private and public areas related to the fundamental principles that shape who they are and what they stand for. What can increase the integrity of an organization or person is moving more information into the public areas. When there is alignment between principles-in-action and espoused principles, individuals and organizations increase their trustworthiness and integrity. Alignment with core principles is improved through feedback, dialogue, and reflection.

Integrity and trustworthiness between individuals exists when what others perceive about each other from behaviors align with what each thinks and says. Distrust exists when one's actions and words are misaligned with his or her espoused principles. In organizations, the incongruence between what the system espouses and how it acts contributes disengagement and even skepticism.

For deep change to occur, educators will want to work at the principle level, helping those engaged in change understand the core principles associated with a change initiative and giving them opportunities as they acquire new behaviors to understand and examine the principles that drive the new actions. "Without understanding the

Three strategies for examining principles

Three strategies for examining principles that guide professional learning in schools or school systems are outlined below. The first process calls for developing a teachable point of view about significant issues related to professional learning and student success. Some of these topics might be how learning happens for adults; how learning for adults is linked to learning for students; how change in practice occurs; what is high-quality professional learning, etc. The second process guides an individual through the process of developing a set of personal principles. The third process guides teams of educators through a process of developing school- or district-level professional development principles.

TEACHABLE POINT OF VIEW

In *Leading for Results: Transforming Teaching, Learning, and Relationships in Schools* (2007), Dennis Sparks describes the process of creating teachable points of view as a way to identify important ideas. Tichy (2002) believes that the act of developing a teachable point of view helps leaders gain clarity about their underlying assumptions about themselves and their organization. Tichy advocates that leaders share their teachable points of view with others in a process he calls "interactive teaching" in which the leader shares his or her point of view with the intention of learning from those who are listening and who know that they can expand and enrich the leader's understanding of his or her own point of view. This cycle continues as the leader continues to refine his or her point of view using what he or she is learning to enrich, clarify, and expand it. In this way the leader is gaining perspective he or she does not have in order to develop a stronger and clearer point of view that will lead the organization forward.

CLARIFYING PERSONAL PRINCIPLES

Dennis Sparks, in a presentation to the Annual Colloquium of the California Staff Development Council, chose to encourage change in an unusual way. Rather than telling the audience what changes he wanted to see and then exhorting them to put them into practice, he engaged them in dialogue. He stated his assumptions and asked those present to clarify their own assumptions and those of others. One assumption Sparks (2004) identified is: "The existing talents and creative potential of educators are a vast and untapped resource" (p. 56).

The process outlined below guides individuals to examine their personal principles about professional learning or about other topics of importance.

- State clearly and concisely the operating principles that guide decisions about professional learning.
- Ask others to share their principles about professional learning.
- Engage in dialogue designed to understand others' perspective rather than to reach consensus or to determine which principles are right or wrong.

- Ask members to share information/ feedback with each other about how their stated principles appear in their actions and words. Avoid identifying ways in which actions are not aligned with principles unless the group agrees to engage in this work collectively and in a supportive, healthy culture.
- Ask each member to formulate a new statement of principle about professional learning that reflects what he or she learned from deep and committed listening to others share their experiences.
- Continue to engage in this form of dialogue until clarity about one's own principles emerge.
- Seek input about the alignment of one's espoused principles and principles-in-action and use that information to adjust to both one's principles and behaviors.

CLARIFYING DISTRICT OR SCHOOL PRINCIPLES

The process described below can be used to clarify a district's or school's principles about professional learning or other topics of interest.

- Ask members of a team to generate statements of their understanding of organizational principles related to professional learning or to review statements of organizational principles about professional learning. Strategic plans frequently include these.
- Ask members to contribute examples of professional development routines, practices, policies, etc., where the principles are manifested and examples where there is incongruence. Members are seeking to determine in this step if the principles are only espoused or are actually principles-in-action. Strong organizations typically have tight alignment between their espoused principles and principles-in-action.
- Examine places where there is dissonance or disagreement. If there is incongruence, members discuss the principles that are foundational to building a trusting community in which all members learn and grow each day and the associated organizational practices, policies, processes, etc., needed to bring alignment and coherence between the desired principles and behaviors.
- Clarify and publicize professional development principles and establish routines, practices, policies, etc., that align with them.
- Monitor the implementation of professional development principles by asking members to review on a continuing basis the alignment between their individual and organization beliefs and routines, practices, policies, to celebrate their application, and to recognize how they contribute to both personal and organizational success.

principles of a given task," says Covey, "people become incapacitated when the situation changes and different practices are required to be successful" (p. 15). "But when we teach practices without principles, we tend to make people dependent on us or others" (p. 25). Our experience tells us that many educational change initiatives fail because leaders focus too much on the actions and insufficiently on the principle level of change. New behaviors are often not sustained over time because beliefs and theories have not been transformed and principles not deeply embedded.

IN PRACTICE

The difficult part of adopting shared principles is determining if espoused principles and principles-in-action align. This is where moving from the private space of the Johari Window can help. If we are open to knowing what is unknown and accept feedback as information, we grow more aware of our principles-in-action and how they impact how we think, speak, and act. This work takes both intentionality and consciousness as well as opportunity to engage in reflection and dialogue to learn about the principles governing our organizations. We embed principles into the organization by clarifying, teaching, and examining them, rather than dwelling exclusively on the practices. When the principles guide the thoughts, actions, and words of members of an organization, they can self-manage, contribute to the well-being of the organization, and feel deeply satisfied with their commitment and integrity.

PRINCIPLES ABOUT PROFESSIONAL LEARNING

What does all this have to do with professional learning? Schools and districts offer a number of examples of principles-in-action contradicting espoused principles. When contradictions exist, unevenness in practice exists and practices that support high-quality professional learning are shallow rather than deeply embedded into the fiber of a school system.

The examples about professional learning on the next page demonstrate how espoused principles, those we speak, and principles-in-action, those we demonstrate through our actions, can be contradictory.

The contradiction between what is said and what is done creates dissonance in a system. This dissonance can be either healthy or unhealthy. Dissonance can be healthy if the system or individuals use the dissonance and move the information from "unknown to self" or "unknown to self and others" to the "known to self" category and use it to align espoused principles and principles-in-action. Dissonance can be unhealthy if it is ignored.

For those who want to make a significant and lasting change in professional learning, examine your principles-in-action, clarifying both personal and organizational principles to guide decisions related to high-quality professional learning. You can use this book to initiate dialogue about principles that are intended to lead the field to a new level of results for educators and, more importantly, for students.

By focusing on guiding principles, this book encourages district, school, and teacher leaders to take three actions. The first action is to examine their current practices of professional development for their underlying principles. The second action is to determine the degree to which espoused principles and principles-in-action align. The third action is to clarify the principles they view as most important and that guide professional development in their school or district. Because schools, districts, agencies, and organizations are at different developmental stages and operate in different policy and contextual arenas, we cannot prescribe practices for them to adopt. What we can do is shine a spotlight on the principles that guide decision making about professional learning and create a vision of effective professional learning for all educators that occurs as part of their daily work. The

principles will serve as the foundation upon which professional learning practices are congruent with standards-based, job-embedded, results-driven professional learning that improves teaching, learning, and leading.

Clarifying an organization's principles takes time and dialogue because each member of the organization brings with

EXAMPLES OF HOW ACTIONS CONTRADICT ESPOUSED PRINCIPLES

Espoused principles (What is said)	Principles-in-action (What is evident)	Evidence in practice (What others see)
Training without follow-up is malpractice.	Educators are held accountable for implementing practices that they learned in training without support or assistance.	Limited or no follow-up opportunities are embedded into the design of professional learning experiences.
Professional learning is an integral component of school improvement.	Professional development workshops are planned and delivered in isolation from school improvement planning and goal setting.	Professional development occurs sporadically throughout the school year or outside the contract day.
Teachers are professionals.	Teachers are technicians, carefully implementing programs of prescriptive curriculum.	Professional development trains all teachers to implement prescriptive behavior with limited variation.
Effective professional learning is measured in terms of its impact on student learning.	Seat time, not application of learning, is rewarded.	States and local school districts have policies that recognize or reward participation based on hours attended rather than evidence of learning.
Professional learning respects and adheres to principles of adult learning.	All adults are expected to comply with the same professional development requirements.	Educators experience one-size-fits-all learning experiences.

Guiding principles

In the Green Bay (Wisc.) Area Public School District, the team working on the comprehensive professional development plan developed a set of guiding principles to drive their work.

Professional learning:
- Is based on an unwavering commitment to student learning.
- Operates on the assumption that all students can and will learn.
- Occurs when planned, implemented, and evaluated collaboratively to improve student learning and teacher effectiveness.
- Reflects best available research and practice in leadership, teaching, learning, and assessment.
- Respects and nurtures the intellectual, reflective, and leadership capacity of the entire school community.
- Promotes continuous improvement based on data and dialogue.
- Is embedded, ongoing, and sustainable in each school and the district.

Used with permission.

him or her personal principles. "It is very difficult to give up our certainties — our positions, our beliefs, our explanations," asserts Wheatley. "These help define us; they lie at the heart of our personal identity. Yet I believe we will succeed in changing this world only if we can think and work together in new ways. Curiosity is what we need. We don't have to let go of what we believe, but we do need to be curious about what someone else believes. We do need to acknowledge that their way of interpreting the world might be essential to our survival" (2002, p. 35).

CONCLUSION

We have come to realize both through practice and through research that professional learning is more important than ever in improving teaching, leading, and learning. Principles shape the nature of the professional learning we experience. This book proposes principles that will lead the next

decade of practice in the field. Rather than being static, we hope these principles will be dynamic and continuously refined and more deeply understood through ongoing dialogue-like conversations (Sparks, 2007) about their implications and the routines, practices, and policies they generate.

The question that looms large as this book begins is the degree to which we are willing to experience dissonance as a means to transform our principles and practices. To what degree are we open to the honest, constructive feedback that allows us to move more from the "unknown to self and others" and "unknown to self" into the "known to self and others" category? How willing are we to know if our espoused principles align with principles-in-action? To what degree are we willing to share observations about discrepancies if they exist and then move to resolve them? To what degree are we willing to engage in dialogue to understand one another's principles? To what degree are we willing to clarify the principles that will govern decision making about professional learning in our school or system? To what degree are we willing to consider professional learning at the principle level and before we introduce professional learning practices?

When practices change without deep exploration of the principles that guide them, people will be pulled back to their old ways. "As we work together to restore hope to the future, we need to include a new and strange ally — our willingness to be disturbed," says Wheatley (2002). "Our willingness to have our beliefs and ideas challenged by what others think. No one person or perspective can give us the answers we need to the problems of today. Paradoxically, we can only find those answers by admitting we don't know. We have to be willing to let go of our certainty and expect ourselves to be confused for a time" (p. 34).

REFERENCES

Argyris, C. (1982). *Reasoning, learning, and action.* San Francisco: Jossey-Bass.

Collins, J. (2001). *Good to great: Why some companies make the leap … and others don't.* New York: Harper Business.

Covey, S. (1991). *Principle-centered leadership.* New York: Simon & Schuster.

Knight, J. (2007). *Instructional coaching: A partnership approach to improving instruction.* Thousand Oaks, CA: Corwin Press.

Luft, J. (1969). *On human interaction.* Palo Alto, CA: National Press.

Oxford English Dictionary. (http://dictionary.oed.com/cgi/entry/ 50188755?query_type=word&queryword=p rinciple&first=1&max_to_show=10&sort_ type=alpha&result_place=2&search_ id=Uwfh-0Csb1d-6129&hilite=50188755) Downloaded March 16, 2007.

Pasi, R. (2003). Introduction to the special issue: Leadership with vision and purpose. *NASSP Bulletin, 87*(637), 1.

Schon, D. (1983). *The reflective practitioner.* New York: Basic Books.

Senge, P. (1990). *The fifth discipline.* New York: Currency Doubleday.

Senge, P., Roberts, C., Ross, R., Smith, B., & Kleiner, A. (1994). *The fifth discipline fieldbook: Strategies and tools for building a learning organization.* New York: Currency Doubleday.

Sparks, D. (2003). Transformational learning. *Journal of Staff Development, 24*(1), 29.

Sparks, D. (2004). A call to creativity. *JSD, 25*(1), 54-62.

Sparks, D. (2007). *Leading for results: Transforming teaching, learning and relationships in schools,* (2nd ed.). Thousand Oaks, CA: Corwin Press and NSDC.

Tichy, N. (2002). *The cycle of leadership: How great leaders teach their companies to win.* New York: Harper Business.

Wheatley, M. (2002). *Turning to one another.* San Francisco: Berrett-Koehler.

"None of us is as smart as all of us."
— *Phil Condit*

PRINCIPLE 2

DIVERSITY

Diversity strengthens an organization
and improves its decisions.

T oday's schools are being asked to achieve something they have never before been asked to achieve — ensure that all students achieve high standards of learning. Educators are committed to the goal that every student graduates and is prepared for post-secondary education or entry into the workforce. In our view, this goal requires educators to work together toward ensuring student success. When educators each contribute what they know to support one another, together they start to solve problems related to how students learn. But it can go much deeper than that. When educators come together to share and learn how to design instruction to meet the unique needs of students and how best to engage and motivate students, they share resources that help students become contributing, productive citizens of the world and address complex issues related to human interaction.Singleton remarks to Sparks (2002), "I believe the goal of schooling is to prepare students to thrive in a multiracial, multiethnic democracy. What that means is not only understanding our own culture, but also having the ability to negotiate unfamiliar cultures" (p. 62).

To embrace this goal and all of its opportunities and challenges, educators will need to reach beyond their own frame of reference and experiences to develop a broad and deep understanding of other people, cultures, and social mores. Diversity in all its forms strengthens learning. In professional development, we recognize the importance of diversity because it enriches the collaborative experience of educators. Diversity brings depth and perspective to collaborative learning, dialogue, and decision making. Diversity of opinions, experiences, family background, race, ethnicity, gender, age, location, sexual orientation, disabilities, lifestyle, and socioeconomic status expands our capacity to fully understand reality, to appreciate differences in perspective, and to make decisions that affect student learning that are appropriate, respectful, and informed. When professional learning intentionally weaves diversity into its very fabric, both systems and individuals benefit from the rich dialogue that leads to better decisions. This principle is powerful because it encourages schools and school systems to tap the richness of its members and to reinforce the collective responsibility for adult and student learning.

Our society typically thinks of diversity in terms of two things: race and culture. In the educational context, the meaning of diversity includes and extends beyond the traditional view. "We know what it is, and we understand that in addition to race and ethnicity," says Graham (2007), "diversity is defined by many other factors, including culture, generations, and perspectives, that can inform and fundamentally improve the dialogue of the organizations we serve. The end results of increased diversity are better decisions, better programs, and better services" (p. 13).

RATIONALE

In education, where there are few absolute solutions to challenges, educators have a greater responsibility to explore extensive and diverse possibilities and perspectives before making a decision or choosing a pathway. When we ensure diversity in members making decisions, we are more confident in the outcome. Diversity among group members during decision making strengthens the quality of the outcome, ownership and commitment to its implementation, and pride in its achievement. In education, the benefit is simple — improved teaching and learning.

Diversity increases the likelihood of ownership and commitment to challenges and opportunities. When individuals see

their perspectives and voices represented and honored during decision making, they are more likely to support the outcomes of the process. For example, a school system working on a new secondary homework policy would normally seek the input of principals, teachers, and counselors. Embracing the principle of diversity means the school system would include the perspectives of parents, students, and businesses in the community that hire students. Bringing together the voices of all individuals and organizations that will be asked to support and comply with any new policy increases the likelihood that the new policy will work for all stakeholders.

Diversity strengthens educators' decisions. The more information and diverse perspectives that can be examined during decision making, the more likely the group will arrive at the best decision. Surowiecki (2005) writes, "The positive case for diversity, as we've seen, is that it expands a group's set of possible solutions and allows the group to conceptualize problems in novel ways" (p. 36). We maximize the diversity of groups involved in education decisions by engaging in the process members with different experience, expertise, perspective, ethnicity, and race. There is additional benefit in engaging individuals with different years of experience in decision-making venues. Educators in early years of their careers have different perspectives from those who have more years of teaching.

Educators also have different perspectives on solutions to problems in education than do parents, nonparent community members, or business people in the community. When their perspectives are added to those of educators, all members have information they would not individually have and gain an understanding of the problem that no individual member can gain. As a result, the team makes better decisions and is far more likely to reap benefits from their decisions.

Different levels of expertise can bring different perspectives to problem solving and decision making. Moving decisions closest to the point of implementation has long been a management strategy that honors and empowers all employees in an organization. Sometimes, though, exposing those closest to the point of implementation to new perspectives, beliefs, or information can help them make even better decisions. ". . . [I]f you can assemble a diverse group of people who possess varying degrees of knowledge and insight," Surowiecki (2005) suggests, "you are better off entrusting it with major decisions rather than leaving them in the hands of one or two people, no matter how smart those people are" (p. 31).

There is richness in the diversity of race, ethnicity, and culture. Regardless of the commitment of a single person or single race team, for example, to be open-minded and to consider the view of all, it is impossible to do so when the actual experiences of the team are limited. As much as a team might be committed to identifying fair and equitable solutions to problems, there will be occasions when it cannot because members' understanding is restricted to their frame of reference. "I am fond of this quotation from the Talmud," acknowledges Graham (2007). " 'We see things not as they are. We see them as we are' " (p. 13). It is rare for anyone to be able to understand all perspectives of an issue.

One of us (Hirsh) experienced how the majority may not recognize a minority experience from the perspective of religion. While serving on her local school board, she was often involved in conversations about school celebrations associated with Christian holidays. These conversations and, even

more so the celebrations, create situations that may be uncomfortable or confusing for non-Christian children. Frequently, Christians failed to acknowledge Jewish and Muslim children's religious holy days or celebrations. While decision makers never intend to make decisions that cause discomfort for some children, decision makers with one perspective, view, or belief system may be unable to anticipate the potential impact of their decisions. When we deliberately involve individuals who expand the experience and understanding of the team, we are more likely to create solutions that serve all children well.

Diversity during decision making accelerates action. We can be comfortable with our decisions when all potential solutions and perspectives have been explored; when all sides of an issue have been thoroughly investigated; when stakeholders have been given multiple opportunities for input and responses; and when decision makers have used a tool like the impact wheel to explore all potential consequences of actions they are considering (Barker, 2006). Decisions that result from this process are easier to explain and for others to understand and accept. While we can't eliminate opposition or resistance, we are better prepared to respond to concerns because most concerns are addressed during decision making. Diversity during decision making eliminates barriers to implementation because those barriers, fears, or excuses are naturally addressed in the process. When decision makers have dealt with all issues related to implementation through diversity among the decision makers, implementation and results are accelerated.

Diversity increases confidence and courage to act. Confidence in our decisions increases enthusiasm, motivation, and encouragement needed to take new actions.

We strengthen decisions regarding teaching and learning when we consider issues related to diversity. We take the necessary time to include voices that are different from ours and craft decisions, plans, and actions that satisfy the interests of the whole community rather than a portion of it. Because educators make many decisions that influence the quality of the teaching and learning students experience each day, these decisions, if crafted through diversity, can provide more opportunity for every student. Through this process, educators, too, discover the richness and value of many different and unique perspectives.

Ultimately, teaching and learning improve when the strength of diversity is recognized in the classroom as well as the boardroom. Surowiecki (2005) adds, "Groups that are too much alike find it harder to keep learning, because each member is bringing less and less new information to the table. Homogenous groups are great at doing what they do well, but they become progressively less able to investigate alternatives" (p. 31). When school leaders embrace this aspect of diversity, then the structures for team learning change. Teams are organized to ensure diversity and avoid groupthink. Teams leverage diversity of memberships to ensure consideration of multiple options, to debate all sides of issues, and to produce the very best plans of actions to serve children well. Teaching and learning are more likely to change as a result of these situations than situations when educators act with good intentions yet don't see other options for achieving the results they seek.

SUPPORTING EVIDENCE

Diversity strengthens educators' decisions. The more information and diverse perspectives that can be examined in the decision-making process, the more likely the group is to arrive at the best decision. Surowiecki (2005) writes, "The positive case for diversity, as we've seen, is that it expands a group's set of possible solutions and allows the group to conceptualize problems in novel ways" (p. 36). We maximize the diversity of groups involved in education decisions by engaging in the process members with different experience, expertise, perspective, ethnicity, and race.

Educators strive each day to narrow achievement gaps, and some have been more successful than others in eliminating them. Yet that success rate is too small. Fortunately, research and anecdotal evidence reinforce the argument that the strengths of diversity can be applied to produce better results for educators and their students.

Many educators are uncomfortable addressing issues of diversity and in many cases struggle with appropriate ways to engage with it. While their goal is respect, many often minimize the importance and contribution of the differences. Most often, they remain silent, letting the critical conversations that are essential remain unheard or heard only among a few in covens of secrecy. "As we have seen, in schools educators tend to group out differences as best they can, as fast as those differences appear — differences in ability, social class, special needs, gender — in the name of promoting teacher performance and pupil achievement," cautions Barth (2001). "My experience in schools suggests that it is maximizing rather than minimizing differences among a group of learners that is associated with the steepest learning curves. Embracing differences supports reflection, learning, and the creation of knowledge" (p. 129). Lambert et al. (2002) write, "Learning is a social activity that is enhanced by shared inquiry. Learners learn with more depth and understanding when they are able to share ideas with others, engage in the dynamic and synergistic process of thinking together, consider other points of view, and broaden their own perspectives" (p. 27).

Porras, Emery, and Thompson (2006) write, "Contention about the issues, if left untapped and without an outlet, will become destructive down the road where it will be unwelcome, personal, and counter-productive. Worse yet, avoiding contention cheats you out of the best opportunity to unlock the most powerful ideas. This is fertile ground at the beginning of every project and a dustbowl if it never gets planted" (p. 190). In an interview with Sparks (2002), Heifetz adds, "In our effort to control the dangers of conflict, we also eradicate the benefits of having different points of view within an organization. Conflict can be a resource that promotes creativity and learning" (p. 46).

Wheatley (2002) offers guidance for structuring conversations that seek diversity of participants and views. "I can't think of anything that's given me more hope recently than to observe how simple conversations that originate deep in our caring give birth to powerful actions that change lives and restore hope to the future," she writes (p. 23). "Here are the principles I've learned to emphasize before we begin a formal conversation process:

- We acknowledge one another as equals;
- We try to stay curious about each other;
- We recognize that we need each other's help to become better listeners;
- We slow down so we have time to think and reflect;
- We remember that conversation is the natural way humans think together; and
- We expect it to be messy at times" (p. 29).

Developing one's own racial identity is also key to being open to the benefits of diversity. Sparks (2004) interviews Beverly Daniel Tatum, who notes "…[W]hen I talk with teachers, I offer several guiding assumptions. One is that all of us have a racial identity to which we may or may not have paid attention. If you are a person of color in our society, it's hard to go very far in your life without someone bringing your racial group membership to your attention. If you are a white person living in a largely white community, you can go a very long time without anyone commenting on your whiteness. A second guiding assumption is that I want people to feel good about their racial identities … A third assumption is that adolescents of color really begin to think about their identities during adolescence . … All of this is happening in the presence of white teachers who have no personal history with that type of identity exploration, nor have they given much thought to their own identities, even in midlife. If one person is having an experience that another has not shared or even thought about, it's easy to see where there can be misunderstanding and conflict" (p. 49).

In the same interview (Sparks, 2004), Tatum emphasizes the important role leaders must play in schools to ensure that diversity is valued. Tatum states, "It is important that leaders model what they want faculty members to do. When leaders openly address issues, they set a context for these discussions. When you are in a leadership role, people pay attention to what you say and do. If leaders believe it is important that everyone in the school community feel included, then they'll be included, then they'll be inclusive in their style of operation" (p. 51).

When teachers and principals have a deep understanding of their own beliefs, attitudes, and expectations regarding race, they create learning experiences in which all students succeed. Singleton and Linton (2006) urge educators to begin their efforts in closing the achievement gap with "an examination of self rather than others … When conversations focus first on educators' own racial consciousness, identity, and experiences, they can better understand the way in which they may be interpreting their students' academic interests and engagement" (p. 73). The authors propose six conditions for having "courageous conversations" about race and social class in which educators engage in the deep reflection and dialogue necessary to challenge their own misconceptions, beliefs, and actions. The conditions are: being aware of one's personal experiences with race; keeping the focus on race as the topic of conversations; seeking multiracial perspectives; keeping everyone engaged in the conversations; understanding race and its history; and understanding whiteness.

A critical step in the process of valuing diversity as defined by Singleton and Linton (2006) is, acquiring the language and communication to be able to engage in "courageous conversations." "In essence," according to the authors, "only when educators establish both a language and process for communication about racial matters will they be poised to restructure their schools, classrooms, curricula, and relationships with students and families in ways that improve student engagement and performance" (p. 71).

IN PRACTICE

NSDC's Equity standard reads as follows: *Staff development that improves the learning of all students prepares educators to understand and appreciate all students, create safe, orderly, and supportive learning environments, and hold high expectations for their aca-*

demic achievement. If diversity is part of the decision making that contributes to the design of learning environments, expectations, and engagement for students, increasingly more students will feel respected, included, and valued. This sense of personal integrity is an important factor in creating an equitable learning experience for each student. We are confident that there is a definitive link between the strength of a school's commitment to equitable expectations and practices and the success of every student.

Hirsh had the opportunity to enroll her children in an elementary school that had once served a segregated black community. Many parents voluntarily bused their children to the school which had been converted to a magnet to avoid court-ordered desegregation. Hirsh wanted her children to experience diversity from a very young age. Hirsh's children, like so many others who have opportunities to experience diversity firsthand, learned to trust, value, and appreciate the diversity of their classmates. Parents, too, learned to work side by side, respecting and acknowledging their differences, on the common goal of ensuring every child's success. Long, heated conversations in which various perspectives were aired frequently characterized site-based decision-making council meetings. At one time, Killion facilitated a meeting among the school staff and community members and helped the staff realize that they all had the same interests, ensuring the success of all children, even though they had different views about how to achieve this result. Over the years, as the tension dissipated and trust and respect grew, the real strength of diversity played out over and over again on the playground, in study hall, in teacher meetings, in classrooms, and in PTA meetings. Ultimately, the U.S. Department of Education noticed as well and awarded the school the Blue Ribbon for Excellence.

Through professional learning, all educators have opportunities to understand their own attitudes regarding race, social class, and culture and how their attitudes affect their teaching practices and expectations for student learning and behavior. In dialogue with colleagues, in book studies, in collaborative planning, etc., educators deepen their own understanding about how their race, social class, and culture influence their decisions, behaviors, and expectations. While high-quality professional learning experiences cannot substitute for authentic background experiences, they can assist in developing an ability to understand and value different perspectives and to use that understanding to make more informed decisions. Effective professional learning can also help educators explore how differences influence relationships with colleagues, students, parents, and the community, as well as contribute to increased sensitivity and empathy as well as a stronger school community.

Talking about race and social class is a first step to acting on what we learn. Wheatley (2002) suggests we begin with conversations. However, she cautions, "Conversation can only take place among equals. If anyone feels superior, it destroys conversation. Words then are used to dominate, coerce, manipulate. Those who act superior can't help but treat others as objects to accomplish their causes and plans. When we see each other as equals, we stop misusing them. We are equal because we are human beings. Acknowledging you as my equal is a gesture of love" (p. 141).

In describing unhealthy cultures in schools, Barth (2001) speaks about the culture of silence. "Nondiscussables are subjects sufficiently important that they are talked about frequently but are so laden with anxiety and fearfulness that these conversations take place only in the parking lot, the rest rooms, the playground, the car pool, or the dinner table at home. We are fearful that open discussion of these incendiary issues in polite society — at a faculty meeting, for example — will cause a meltdown. The nondiscussable is the elephant in the living room. Everyone knows this huge pachyderm is there, right between the sofa and the fireplace, and we go on mopping and dusting and vacuuming around it as if it did not exist" (p. 9). Conversations about diversity in schools are elephants many are unwilling to name.

Singleton and Linton (2006) share the story about how Chapel Hill-Carrboro City Schools in North Carolina, worked to discuss the nondiscussables. The white superintendent, Neil Pederson, and black assistant superintendent, Nettie Collins-Hart, worked hand in hand to lead the "courageous conversations" Singleton and Linton talk about. The authors quote Collins-Hart:

"We really had to begin to look at the things we hadn't talked about and race, in a very sensitive and direct way, was the one thing we hadn't dealt with. ... I think at first the biggest challenge for me personally was getting used to the idea that we were actually going to talk candidly about race. But the next hurdle was developing some skills to talk about it, such as having the same basis of vocabulary and having a similar understanding of race, because it is not something people do naturally, and in interracial groups particularly" (pp. 128-129).

Grant and Wong (2004) write about their experience with an incredibly diverse educational situation and the success its students experienced. "When we first encountered the multilingual/multiethnic school communities of Tulip Valley and Powhatan Elementary, our goal was to identify the qualities of leadership that helped to establish their reputations as schools where language minority students were successful. Also, we wanted to learn about the effective strategies and practices used to encourage parental involvement. On reflection, we realize now that we have learned so much more. Through professional development, teacher consciousness, attitudes, and behaviors regarding language minority students were reconstructed. As the teachers replaced deficit perspectives about language differences with culturally sensitive models, they improved communication with their language minority students, strengthened teaching, and became better advocates for their students" (p. 22).

Guerra and Nelson (2007) call on school leaders to create culturally proficient organizations. They say culturally proficient organizations have policies and practices that enable people to interact effectively in environments that are diverse. Noguera (1999) writes, "… though the number of cases is small, there are schools where no achievement gap exists, and there are students who achieve at high levels despite the incredible odds against them. These bright spots of success provide us with a window through which we can examine what might be possible …" (p. 6).

CONCLUSION

Each day educators in schools, regardless of where they are, experience diversity. Sometimes, the diversity is in race and ethnicity. Sometimes, it is in learning style. Sometimes, it is in family structure, or gender, or gender orientation, or economic status, or level of achievement. Educators meet diversity in language and cognitive, emotional, and physical needs. Each day, every school, every classroom is a place where diversity strengthens an opportunity

to learn by understanding the world from a different perspective. When educators remain silent or hold conversations in private, when they fear discussing nondiscussables, or when they lack a deep understanding of their own identity, children lose opportunities to learn.

Ferguson (2007) notes that schools, like our nation, are becoming more diverse. "The nation's future will depend on how effectively schools and teachers respond" (p. 33) to the increase in nonwhite students and those with language differences. Teachers, he says, will need tools, technology, and techniques to support student learning. " … Future professional learning experiences should equip teachers with the knowledge and technology to manage classrooms more effectively and to scaffold instruction for students who arrive with different types and levels of preparation" (p. 33).

Just as Lincoln gathered around him his political rivals to strengthen his party and eventually form a cabinet (Goodwin, 2006), educators engage those whose views and experiences differ so that we can make sound educational decisions for all students. This takes more than the invitation to join the conversations. It takes the commitment and investment in learning to expand our own narrow understanding. "As we work together to restore hope to the future," says Wheatley (2002), "we need to include a new and strange ally — our willingness to be disturbed" (p. 34). Inviting diverse perspectives into our decision making for professional learning will give us the greatest degree of confidence that we will make the best decisions on behalf of educators, adults, and children.

REFERENCES
Barth, R. (2001). *Learning by heart.* San Francisco: Jossey-Bass.

Barker, J. (2006, December 4). *New skills for exploring the future.* Keynote address to NSDC Annual Conference, Nashville, TN.

Ferguson, R. (2007). Becoming more sophisticated about diversity. *JSD, 28*(3), 33.

Goodwin, D.K. (2006). *Team of rivals: The political genius of Abraham Lincoln.* New York: Simon & Schuster.

Graham IV, J. (2007, February). The efforts of inclusion. *Association Now, 3*(2), 13.

Grant, R.A. & Wong, S.D. (2004). Forging multilingual communities: School-based strategies. *Multicultural Perspectives, 6*(3), 17-23.

Guerra, P. & Nelson, S. (2007). Cultural proficiency: Assessment is the first step to creating a school that educates everyone. *JSD, 28*(3), 59-60.

Lambert, L., Walker, D., Zimmerman, D., & Cooper, J. (2002). *The constructivist leader* (2nd ed.). New York: Teachers College Press.

Noguera, P. (1999, April 10). Confronting the challenge of diversity in education. *InMotion Magazine,* www.inmotion-magazine.com/pndivers.html

Porras, J., Emery, S., & Thompson, M. (2006). *Success built to last: Creating a life that matters.* Upper Saddle River, NJ: Wharton School Publishing.

Singleton, G. & Linton, C. (2006). *Courageous conversations about race: A field guide for achieving equity in schools.* Thousand Oaks, CA: Corwin Press.

Sparks, D. (2002). Bringing a spirit of invention to leadership: An interview with Ron Heifetz. *Journal of Staff Development, 23*(2), 44-46.

Sparks, D. (2004). How to have conversations about race: An interview with Beverly Daniel Tatum. *JSD, 25*(4), 48-52.

Sparks, D. (2002). Conversations about race need to be fearless: An interview with Glenn Singleton. *Journal of Staff Development, 23*(4), 60-64.

Surowiecki, J. (2005). *The wisdom of crowds.* New York: Anchor.

Wheatley, M. (2002). *Turning to one another: Simple conversations to restore hope to the future.* San Francisco: Berrett-Koehler.

"Leaders matter."

— Dennis Sparks

PRINCIPLE 3

LEADERSHIP

Leaders are responsible for building the capacity
in individuals, teams, and organizations
to be leaders and learners.

Little debate exists about the importance of strong leadership as a core feature of success in schools and school districts. Research for nearly three decades has recognized that leaders do matter. This principle has two components. The first is who leads. Leaders exist throughout the system. If leadership rests in the hands of an elite few, little deep and sustainable change will occur. The second is what leaders do. Leaders at the district, school, and classroom level contribute to improving student learning. Senge (2006) argues that "leadership for deep change requires replacing the myth of the 'hero leader' with the concept of leadership communities. These communities, he believes, enable the building of leadership capacity throughout the organization so the organization can continually adapt and re-invent itself" (Sparks, 2002). Students will reap substantial rewards when leaders share responsibility for leading, recognize and build on the unique contribution of each person, and focus their efforts on quality teaching and learning. And, more importantly, when all leaders learn, students learn.

Leadership, according to Barth (2001), is "making happen what you believe in" (p. 446). Elmore (2000) describes leadership as "the guidance and direction of instructional improvement" (p. 13). Mintzberg (2004) offers another view:

"Leadership is not about making clever decisions. . . It is about energizing other people to make good decisions and do better things. In other words, it is about helping people release the positive energy that exists naturally within people. Effective leadership inspires more than it empowers; it connects more than it controls; it demonstrates more than it decides. It does all this by *engaging* [italics the author's] — itself above all, and consequently others" (p. 143).

As leaders, teachers, principals, and

central office staff assume a significant responsibility to learn and support their colleagues' learning as their primary approach to improve student learning. "The primary responsibility of all school leaders," asserts Hargreaves and Fink (2003), "is to sustain learning. Leaders of learning put learning at the center of everything they do. They put student learning first, and everyone else's learning is directed toward supporting student learning" (p. 695). What leaders think and do and how they interact with others have a profound effect on how others think, act, and interact. They influence attitudes, actions, and accomplishments.

When all leaders learn, students learn. "Leading for learning means creating powerful, equitable learning opportunities for students, professionals, and the system, and motivating or compelling participants to take advantage of these opportunities," suggest Knapp, Copland, and Talbert (2003, p. 12). Leaders, regardless of their role in the educational system make learning the focus of their work because they hold a belief that when adults learn, students will as well. They continue, "Leaders establish a public, persistent focus on learning by making it central to their own work; consistently communicating that student learning is the shared mission of students, teachers and administrators, and the community; articulating core values that support a focus on powerful, equitable learning; and paying public attention to teaching" (p. 14). Building a system of support for student and professional learning requires, according to Wagner et al. (2006), "leaders whose expertise is more invested in helping a group create the shared knowledge necessary for sustained improvement than in being the certain source of the answers and solution" (p. 209).

Leaders make countless decisions every day that have the potential to improve student learning. When they use their own learning, the learning of colleagues, and student learning as the primary criterion for those decisions, they leverage their role as leaders to develop a learning system. From our perspective, building the capacity of individuals and organizations to learn and lead is the most important responsibility leaders have. When leaders realize the crucial link between their leadership and learning and student learning, they will engage in powerful behaviors that serve as the core of leadership. The "line in the sand" for leaders of learning is the degree to which each decision influences student learning, focuses the leader's time and efforts on impacting student learning, and merits the leader's attention.

Leaders have a responsibility to exhibit instructional leadership by considering every decision and action through the lens of whether it positively impacts student learning; and to recognize that their own learning is paramount to effective leadership. They also must build the leadership capacity of everyone within the school community so that leadership is not reserved for one person but leveraged best when shared with others and acknowledge that sharing leadership widely increases others' sense of personal and collective responsibility for student learning results.

RATIONALE

Leaders throughout the educational system are responsible for learning. Key to Knapp, Copland, and Talbert's (2003) assertions "about leading for learning is the notion that leaders not only set the stage for learning, they also take concrete steps along pathways that lead to student, professional, and system learning. In this sense, leaders can exert a direct and identifiable influence on learning results" (p. 13). Leaders lead learning and share responsibility for leading. They model learning and shape the organization's culture so that it supports learning. They share responsibility for learning and leading and they ensure the system is learning. They coach others toward excellence, they provide resources, they hold a vision of success and high expectations, and they build trusting relationships and lead with influence rather than coercion. Finally, they hold learning among their top priorities and allocate time and resources to it.

Leadership is shared by virtually everyone who makes decisions related to the primary purpose of schools — student learning. Some hold the assumption that when everyone leads, chaos ensues. Contrary to that is the notion that when everyone shares the vision, has clarity about the organization's goals, and makes collective and individual decisions with the best interests of students in mind, the organization is stronger and more adaptable. Leaders believe that learning is the primary strategy engaging everyone as a leader and for achieving shared goals.

In addition to leading learning, leaders share leadership and responsibility for learning. When principals distribute leadership among teachers, teachers naturally step into leadership roles and commit to the responsibility associated with shared leadership. When central office staff relinquishes to school-based leaders key decisions about a school's goals and the pathway to achieving those goals, interventions are often more focused on the unique nature of the school and its students and staff. When teachers' voices shape the nature of professional learning, their learning is deeply connected to their classroom work, students' learning needs, and the curriculum they teach. When principals can turn to central office

for specific support and resources to accomplish their school's improvement goals, they have greater confidence and a strong sense of efficacy about their goals.

In its Standards for Staff Development, NSDC recognizes the importance of leaders who guide learning. "Leaders at all levels recognize quality professional development as the key strategy for supporting significant improvements. They are able to articulate the critical link between improved student learning and the professional learning of teachers. They ensure that all stakeholders — including the school board, parent teacher organizations, and the business community — understand the link and develop the knowledge necessary to serve as advocates for high-quality professional development for all staff" (2001, p. 10).

Lambert's view of leadership as a community-wide process emphasizes that all members of the community share in both the responsibility and accountability of the success of the school. "By participants, we mean all members of the educational community, not segregated as leaders and followers. At any given time, roles and behaviors will shift among participants based on interest, expertise, experience, and responsibility" (1995, p. 39). "School leadership," adds Lambert (1998), "needs to be a broad concept that is separated from person, role, and discrete individual behaviors. It needs to be embedded in the school community as a whole. Such a broadening of the concept of leadership suggests shared responsibility for a shared purpose of community" (p. 5).

Leaders' success comes when they build leadership capacity within others and within the systems in which they work. Leaders at all levels of the educational system have responsibility to cascade the knowledge, skills, dispositions, and behaviors of successful leadership throughout the system. When teachers engage students in decisions about their learning, when coaches help teachers learn to be effective members of collaborative work teams, when principals distribute leadership responsibilities throughout the staff, when central office creates learning communities for aspiring leaders, novice leaders, and experienced leaders, and when schools and districts create authentic internships, they are developing leaders. The sustaining change means sustaining leadership and spreading it widely throughout the system.

SUPPORTING EVIDENCE

Decades of research confirm that leaders significantly impact the success of their organizations. Not only does it matter who leads, but what they do also matters. Examples of how leaders influence results abound in business, politics, education, and other fields. In synthesizing research about educational leadership practices, Reeves (2006) identifies three significant findings:

- "Leadership, teaching, and adult actions matter" (p. xxii).
- Some leadership actions show "demonstrable links to improved student achievement and educational equity" (p. xxii). These, he reports, include inquiry, implementation, and monitoring.
- "Leadership is neither a unitary skill set nor a solitary activity" (p. xxiv).

Research confirms that some leadership behaviors are more significant than others in supporting professional and student learning. Not all leadership behaviors produce the same effects. Leaders have a significant responsibility to ensure that they and all other leaders practice the leadership behaviors that make the greatest difference in a

school or district. Some of these behaviors are described below.

District Leadership

In meta-analyses of the impact of district leadership behavior on student achievement, Waters and Marzano at Mid-Continent Research for Education and Learning (2006) discovered a positive relationship between superintendent practices and student learning. This suggests that superintendents, through their leadership practices, can influence student learning even though they are removed from the classrooms where teaching and learning actually occur. Waters and Marzano conclude that leadership at the top matters, that effective superintendents create goal-oriented organizations, and that the longer superintendents remain, the more likely they are to positively influence student learning. "These findings suggest that when the district leaders are carrying out their leadership responsibilities effectively, student achievement across the district is positively affected" (p. 11). Waters and Marzano conclude, "We have found a substantial and positive relationship between district-level leadership and student achievement when the superintendent, district office staff, and school board members do the 'right work' in the 'right way.' These findings suggest that superintendents, district office staff, and school board members can contribute to school and student success when they are focused on fulfilling key leadership responsibilities and pursuing practices reported in this study" (p. 20).

Specific district-level leadership behaviors that correlate with student academic success include goal-setting processes, non-negotiable goals for achievement and instruction, board alignment with and support of district goals, monitoring the goals for achievement and instruction, and uses of resources to support the goals for achievement and instruction" (Waters & Marzano, 2006, p. 11). Whether these district leaders are curriculum coordinators, instructional specialists, staff development specialists, the director of human resources, or the director of facilities, their actions, when focused on improving teaching and learning, make a difference in what students, teachers, and principals experience each day.

Because deep change in educational systems can typically take three to five years (Fullan, 2007), leaders intent on making a difference recognize they must take the long view and work through all the parts that must change in order to produce a new framework to sustain the change. These changes include focusing on instruction, standards for performance, resources to support learning, and capacity building. "Sustaining high-quality leadership at the district level is essential to creating supportive conditions for reform," say Datnow and Castellano (2003, p. 188).

When district leaders view sharing leadership and learning as their core responsibility, they convey the value of interdependence, continuous improvement, and high expectation for results. They hold themselves and others responsible for achieving high levels of results and empower everyone in the system to gain the knowledge, develop the skills, and adopt dispositions necessary to ensure that each student is successful. Once that mind-set is achieved, district leaders will then be more willing to commit resources to ensure that all educators learn whatever is necessary to ensure student success.

Principal Leadership

As with district leaders, researchers have concluded that some principal behaviors impact student learning more than others. This is what distinguishes instructionally-focused principals from management-oriented leaders. Cotton's (2003) extensive study of 26 principal leadership behaviors that are related to student achievement identified crucial actions principals take each day. "Principals' behaviors," she concluded, "have little direct impact on student outcomes but substantial indirect impact — that is, impact mediated through teachers and others" (p. 73). Some of the behaviors she identified as influencing student achievement included:

- Establishing with others a vision and goals focused on high levels of student learning.
- High expectations for student achievement.
- Visibility and accessibility.
- Positive, supportive school climate, shared leadership/decision making, and staff empowerment.
- Collaboration.
- Norms of continuous improvement.
- Instructional leadership.

In a more recent study, Marzano, Waters, and McNulty (2005) identified 21 school leader responsibilities that are correlated with student academic achievement. "The data from our meta-analysis demonstrate that there is, in fact, a substantial relationship between leadership and student achievement. We found that the average effect size (expressed as a correlation) between leadership and student achievement is .25" (p. 3).

The leadership responsibilities that Marzano, Waters, and McNulty (2005) identify align with those identified by Cotton (2003). Responsibilities with the highest correlation to student achievement include:

- Situational awareness of what is occurring within the school and having the ability to use this information to identify and solve problems and prevent others;

- Flexibility that adapts leadership behaviors to the needs of the situation;
- Discipline that protects teachers from potential distractions;
- Monitoring and evaluating school practices and their impacts on student learning; and
- Reaching out to the community and acting as an advocate to all stakeholders.

Closely following these responsibilities are culture, order, resources, input, change agent, knowledge of curriculum, instruction, and assessment.

Teacher Leadership

Teacher leadership, according to York-Barr and Duke (2004), is the "process by which teachers, individually or collectively, influence their colleagues, principals, and other members of the school communities to improve teaching and learning practices with the aim of increasing student learning and achievement" (pp. 287-288). "... You don't have to be or to become a principal or superintendent in order to influence the course of a vessel — or a school," asserts Barth (2001). "Indeed, rank in the hierarchy has little relevance when it comes to school-based reform" (p. 78).

Teachers in successful schools collaborate with their peers about teaching and learning. They take a more active role in governance of the school as principals distribute leadership more widely throughout the school. They serve on school improvement teams and share a heightened sense of responsibility and accountability for the success of students in their classrooms and throughout the school.

Teacher leaders fall into three catego-ries, those who lead from their position within the classroom; those who lead from a role outside the classroom, such as coaches or instructional specialists; and those who lead from a formal leadership role, such as department chairs or grade-level or team leaders (Silva, Gimbert, & Nolan, 2000). Regardless of which category teachers are in, they exert significant influence over the success of their students and over the success of their peers. This influence occurs in simple acts such as sharing instructional ideas or resources or in more complex tasks such as serving as a facilitator of a critical friends group.

The benefits of teacher leadership are substantial. York-Barr and Duke (2004) suggest that focusing at the classroom level rather than organizational level produces greater results. "Teacher leadership work that is focused at the classroom level of practices (e.g. implementing instructional strategies) is likely to show student effects more readily than work that is focused at the organizational level (e.g., participating in site-based decision making" (p. 288). They cite four specific benefits of teacher leadership including increased participation by teachers; increased expertise about teaching and learning; opportunities for accomplished teachers to receive recognition and additional professional challenges; and increased student learning.

Murphy (2005) sees benefits of teacher leadership reaching beyond individual teachers in leadership roles to other teachers to the teaching profession to school, and to students. "Murphy proposes a model of embedded logic of teacher leadership," say Killion and Harrison (2006). "In his model, he links teacher professionalism, school health, and classroom and school improvement. What his synthesis of research suggests is that teacher leadership influences teachers' sense of professionalism including their empowerment, commitment, and view of their work as a profession rather than a job." They continue, "In addition, teacher leadership influences the school's culture including the degree to which teachers engage in collegial professional learning and have a strong sense of internal accountability" (pp. 17-18). Teacher leaders influence both school improvement and student learning.

IN PRACTICE

Leaders have multiple ways of leading learning. The examples that follow represent ways leaders, regardless of where they are in the leadership community, improve both the culture for learning and student, professional, and system learning.

A leader is someone who builds the capacity of his or her colleagues. Ed Wittchen, superintendent of Northern Lights School Division in Alberta, Canada, models leadership for learning. He believes in the potential of his employees, coordinates powerful learning experiences for them, partners them with colleagues to reinforce the importance of collaborative learning, and holds high expectations for them. For eight years, Wittchen has sent a contingent of four to eight principals and central office staff members to participate in NSDC's Academy for Staff Developers. He engages his principals in ongoing book talks so that when his principals show up at an NSDC conference, they almost always have a book tucked under their arm. He has invested heavily in helping his school leaders learn about and implement professional learning communities in their schools. He considers his principals' team a learning community and engages them as such in their meetings. What is amazing about Wittchen's work is that he does this in a school district that spans across 300 miles (Richardson, 2005).

A study of principals in high-achieving Georgia schools found that principals more frequently share opportunities for learning with their staff members and support them in participating in learning. When leaders expect learning, hold their colleagues and staff to high expectations for continuous improvement through professional development plans and/or supervision, teachers and students benefit (Baird & Weathersby, 1999).

Courageous leaders work collaboratively with their communities and with their partners to find creative ways to build a school day that supports daily professional learning and collaboration among teams of teachers. District leaders in Carman-Ainsworth School District, in Flint, Mich., worked collaboratively with the district's union leaders over three years through their interest-based bargaining processes and crafted a school week and year that embedded ongoing professional learning within the school day so that all teachers could engage in collaborative, focused professional learning. The importance of professional learning became a whole system focus, not one for a few leaders in central office. Teachers and principals in Carman-Ainsworth have opportunities to learn how to structure their collaborative time effectively and efficiently and assess the results of their work, and have widespread support from colleagues, the community, and the district (Richardson, 2007a).

Richardson (2007b) describes a leadership success story that exemplifies this principle.

Principal Dot Schoeller of Simonton Elementary School in Lawrenceville, Ga., has invested heavily in school-based staff developers — teachers who are released from teaching responsibilities to provide on-the-job learning for other teachers. Schoeller found money in her building budget to support 19 coaches in math and reading. This enables her 197 teachers to meet regularly with a coach to study curriculum and develop lesson plans. Coaches also present model lessons and offer feedback to teachers after observing them teach. Simonton is that rare school that has closed the gap between black and white students in reading. In 2006-07, 86.5% of Simonton's black students were proficient in reading compared to 82.3% of white students. In math, 82.3% of black students met the standard compared to 83.9% of white students. In addition, students with disabilities and English language learners jumped more than 20 percentage points in both math and reading.

Schoeller's willingness to share leadership and focus on student learning demonstrates, as Krajewski (2001) suggests, that "When leaders dream, the 'achievement gap' shrinks. When leaders dream, staff and students are motivated to do better. When leaders dream, school quality increases" (p. 2).

Norfolk (Va.) Public Schools also demonstrates the impact that leadership can make in a school district. "Norfolk Public Schools includes many highly mobile Navy families, and more than half its students are eligible for free or reduced-price lunch," says Zavadsky (2006) in her description of this district's journey to win the Broad Prize, a prestigious honor awarded to urban districts that improve student achievement and close the achievement gap. The district embarked on a program to transform itself from a low-achieving district into a high-achieving district by focusing on culture, extensive professional development, communication, support, and collaboration.

Central office, principals, and teachers joined forces to lead this extensive reform. Principals used data to pinpoint student-learning needs. Norfolk teachers

created a common curriculum across the district's 35 elementary schools, nine middle schools, and five high schools. Instructional specialists worked directly in classrooms to coach teachers, or worked with groups of teachers during grade-level planning time and with school principals to analyze data, identify areas for focus, and set target goals. Teachers met in teams at least twice a week during the workday to plan instruction and review data. Central office administrators and teacher teams conducted regular walk-throughs so the teams could observe how well teachers were meeting district objectives.

Norfolk's results on standardized tests demonstrate higher levels of achievement than demographically similar districts in Virginia, and it narrowed the achievement gap between black and white students. In middle school mathematics, for example, the gap shrank by 9 percentage points between 2001 and 2004.

Killion and Harrison (2006) identify 10 distinctly different roles teacher leaders fill in schools. They include resource provider, data coach, instructional specialist, curriculum specialist, mentor, learning facilitator, classroom supporter, school leaders, catalyst for change, and learner. Some roles are more closely aligned with classroom-level work and others with organizational-level work. The roles provide clarity about possible roles for teacher leaders, flexibility in the contributions they make to their schools, and permit more teachers to assume leadership roles. Each role is unique and built on a distinct set of skills and body of knowledge teacher leaders use in their practice.

CONCLUSION

Leaders make a difference. Yet not all leadership practices have the same degree of impact on performance and results. We have learned from our experiences, research, and a study of practice that students and staff thrive when leaders, regardless of where they are within a school system, focus on student learning, commit to their own professional learning and the learning of others, build strong relationships, shape a collaborative culture, muster resources, and hold a vision for success. "The new model of a school [district] leader is one who is continually learning. The leader's task is allowing people throughout the organization to deal productively with the critical issues they face and to develop mastery in learning disciplines" (NAESP, p. 9). With learning as the main focus for leaders, schools and systems engage in inquiry, solve challenging problems, and share responsibility for the success of one another and every student.

There is a substantial dearth of instructional leadership in schools today, even though research has demonstrated how essential it is to student and teacher success, and that gap must be filled with the brightest minds in the field. "Our nation's schools need nothing less than a new cohort of school principals [teacher leaders, central office administrators, and community leaders] entering our profession," says Barth (2001), "who value and trust learning from experience for themselves and who know how to rigorously and courageously craft school experiences so they will yield important personal learning for adults and students alike. Needed now is the courage — and heart — to think and act otherwise in order to introduce into the schoolhouse a culture hospitable to human learning" (p. 141).

REFERENCES

Baird, R. & Weathersby, J. (1999). *Are changes needed in staff and professional development programs in Georgia?: Issue paper to the governor's education reform study commission: Accountability committee.*

Barth, R. (2001). *Learning by heart.* San Francisco: Jossey-Bass.

Cotton, K. (2003). *Principals and student achievement: What the research says.* Alexandria, VA: ASCD.

Datnow, A. & Castellano, M. (2003). Success for all: District and school leadership. In Murphy, J. & Datnow, A. (2003). *Leadership lessons from comprehensive school reforms*, pp. 187-208, Thousand Oaks, CA: Corwin Press.

Elmore, R. (2000). *Building a new structure for school leadership.* Washington, DC: Albert Shanker Institute.

Fullan, M. (2007). *The new meaning of educational change* (4th ed.). New York: Teachers College Press.

Hargreaves, A. & Fink, D. (2003). Sustaining leadership. *Phi Delta Kappan, 84*(9), 693-700.

Killion, J. & Harrison, C. (2006). *Taking the lead: New roles for teachers and school-based coaches.* Oxford, OH: NSDC.

Knapp, M.S., Copland, M., & Talbert, J.E. (2003, February). *Leading for learning: Reflective tools for school and district leaders.* Seattle, WA: University of Washington, Center for the Study of Teaching and Policy.

Krajewski, B. (2001, April). Introduction to the special section. Closing the achievement gap. *NASSP Bulletin, 85*(624), 2.

Lambert, L. (1998). *Building leadership capacity in schools.* Alexandria, VA: ASCD.

Lambert, L., Walker, D., Zimmerman, D., Cooper, J., Lambert, M., Gardner, M., & Slack, P. (1995). *The constructivist leader.* New York: Teachers College Press.

Marzano, R., Waters, T. & McNulty, B. (2005). *School leadership that works:*

From research to results. Alexandria, VA: ASCD and McREL.

Mintzberg, H. (2004). *Managers not MBAs*. San Francisco: Berrett-Koehler.

Murphy, J. (2005). *Connecting teacher leadership to school improvement*. Thousand Oaks, CA: Corwin Press.

National Association of Elementary School Principals. (2001). *Leading learning communities: Standards for what principals should know and be able to do.* Alexandria, VA: Author.

National Staff Development Council. (2001). *NSDC's standards for staff development, revised*. Oxford, OH: Author.

Reeves, D. (2006). *The learning leader: How to focus school improvement for better results*. Alexandria, VA: ASCD.

Richardson, J. (2005). Relationships and teamwork lead to success. *The Learning System, 1*(1), 1, 6-7.

Richardson, J. (2007a). Bargaining time: Union contract spells out how and when professional learning will happen. *The Learning System, 2*(6), 1, 6-7.

Richardson, J. (2007b). Principal draws up a game plan for school coaches. *The Learning Principal*, 2(4), 1, 6-7.

Senge, P. (2006). *The fifth discipline: The art and practice of learning organizations.* New York: Doubleday Publishing.

Silva, D., Gimbert, B., & Nolan, J. (2000). Sliding the doors: Locking and unlocking possibilities for teacher leadership. *Teachers College Record, 102*(4), 779-806.

Sparks, D. (2002). *Designing powerful professional development for teachers and principals*. Oxford, OH: NSDC.

Wagner, T., Kegan, R., Lahey, L., Lemons, R., Ganier, J., Helsing, D., Howell, A., & Rasmussen, H. (2006). *Change leadership: A practical guide to transforming our schools*. San Francisco: Jossey-Bass.

Waters, T. & Marzano, R. (2006). *School district leadership that works: The effect of superintendent leadership on student achievement — A working paper.* Aurora, CO: McREL.

York-Barr, J. & Duke, K. (2004). What do we know about teacher leadership? Findings from two decades of scholarship. *Review of Educational Research, 74*(3), 255-316.

Zavadsky, H. (2006). Path to excellence: Broad Prize tips. *JSD, 27(*4), 26-29.

"By reaching for what appears to be the impossible,
we often actually do the impossible."
— Jack Welch

PLANNING

Ambitious goals lead to powerful actions
and remarkable results.

Over the years, we have debated a number of issues related to planning for professional learning. We have addressed: What plans should we write? Who should be included in the professional development planning process? What are the critical components of effective plans? At what levels are plans written? But the most important question might be: How do we ensure the plans we write produce the outcomes we seek? Our responsibility to the children in school today makes satisfaction with mediocre or incremental improvement unacceptable. We must strive for planning efforts that produce monumental results. We must dream big because only our most compelling visions will enable us to achieve our greatest results.

On May 25, 1961, in an address to a joint session of Congress on urgent national needs, President John F. Kennedy called for putting a man on the moon before the end of the decade. "I believe that this nation should commit itself to achieving the goal, before this decade is out, of landing a man on the moon and returning him safely to the Earth," he proposed. "No single space project in this period will be more impressive to mankind, or more important for the long-range exploration of space; and none will be so difficult or expensive to accomplish," acknowledged Kennedy. Congress devoted more than $9 billion in the 1960s to this effort. On July 20, 1969, Apollo 11 commander Neil Armstrong stepped out of the lunar lander onto the surface of the moon, signifying that humankind had the intellectual capacity to accomplish significant challenges driven by bold, audacious goals.

High expectations increase results. Wood (2002) writes, "Administrative expectations deeply influence the daily decisions of teachers and other staff members, as well as their approach to long-range planning" (p. 547). Porras, Emery, and Thompson

(2007) write: "In *Built to Last,* Collins and Porras coined the phrase Big Hairy Audacious Goals (BHAGs) to describe how visionary organizations drive boldly toward their aspirations based on their core values. BHAGs don't just exist in parallel to your ideology; they are manifestations of it. They are extensions of who you are and what matters to you" (p. 170).

Professional learning takes on new meaning when educators recognize the important contributions it is expected to make toward the achievement of district and school goals. Schools that are serious about their promise to all children to be successful look for new ways to meet that promise. In many cases, educators themselves and the knowledge and skills they bring to the classroom are the key to keeping the promise. And yet many educators are not equipped to meet the challenges they face in classrooms and are unable to keep their promise and contribute to the big goal. It is at this moment when educators commit to the goal and recognize that they need strategies for achieving it and that professional learning must step up to move educators forward. These conditions place new expectations on professional learning and call for new ways of thinking. Professional learning takes on new importance and high-quality professional learning can deliver.

RATIONALE

We address the importance of ambitious goal setting to ensure professional learning successfully helps all educators and students learn and perform at high levels. Plans mean very little if they are developed in isolation of high expectations and accountability for results. Staff development plans that produce meaningful outcomes are launched by systems that hold the planners responsible for results and empower

them to find meaningful actions. Without high expectations and accountability for results, any action suffices as evidence of progress.

We do not focus on the process or components of staff development plans but rather we would like to contribute a planning process that helps a district achieve its goals for educators and students. For many years, staff development directors and staff development teams created elaborate plans outlining numerous professional development opportunities for staff that produced limited impact in the system or schools.

There are many plausible explanations for why districts experience limited results from elaborate planning processes. Some exert massive attention to planning and lose interest when attention turns to implementation. In these districts, the act of planning — not the outcome — is the priority. In other instances, educators may devote incredible resources to developing a plan and delegate the responsibility of implementation to others who may be less invested in it. The implementers may care more about completing tasks than achieving results.

What distinguishes plans that produce the results we seek and those that get filed when the development work is complete? Our experience has taught us that the process begins with ambitious goal setting that leads to new ways of thinking.

High expectations stimulate great thinking.

Breul (2006) writes: "Stretch goals aim to achieve breakthrough results and always seem impossible at the time you set them. If they seemed reasonable, they would not qualify as stretch or breakthrough goals" (p. 10).

"A stretch goal is an ambitious goal that you don't know how to reach. It is something you have not done before and that you do not know how you are going to achieve. It forces you to discard comfortable solutions and adopt new solutions. A stretch goal communicates that maintaining the status quo is not an option — it cannot be met by tweaking the existing system" (Breul, p. 10).

Stretch goals are similar to BHAGs. Collins and Porras (2002) write: "Like (President Kennedy's) moon mission, a true BHAG is clear and compelling and serves as a unifying focal point of effort — often creating immense team spirit" (p. 94). "A BHAG engages people — it reaches out and grabs them in the gut. It is tangible, energizing, highly focused. People 'get it' right away; it takes little or no explanation. It has a clear finish line, so the organization can know when it has achieved the goal; people like to shoot for finish lines" (p. 94). Calling for all black males to read on grade level by age 10 is an example of a stretch goal for a school system.

Examples of the impact of stretch goals are prevalent in other fields. An international organization committed to the eradication of hunger worldwide called RESULTS operates from the assumption that the resources currently exist to ensure that no child goes to bed hungry and the only thing preventing food from reaching the hungry is the political will to reallocate resources. In 1997, RESULTS set a goal of serving 100 million people by micro credits by 2005. In a 2005 interview, Sam Daley-Harris, founder of RESULTS, reported: "At the time, critics were incredulous and even scornful. Yet, albeit a year later, the micro credits movement anticipates reaching that goal this year (2006, p. 1). Many thought RESULTS was foolish to set such a goal and feared such an ambitious goal would alienate its supporters. Instead, within nine years, 83 million families had been served.

In retrospect, the organizers felt that if they had never set a 100 million goal, they would never have served 83 million. Imagine if they had set a goal of only 10 million.

In 1961, NASA engineers did not have the immediate answer to Kennedy's goal, but they were motivated by the commitment of the nation to achieving it. Similarly, RESULTS volunteers went to work with a passion to find a way to make the goal a reality. We believe that educators can be stimulated to think in new ways when given the challenge of a stretch goal. Imagine what could happen when districts adopt stretch goals that bring attention to issues that have a profound impact on a nation's children. Imagine the sense of responsibility felt by educators who sit with a superintendent and school board members to set their district's goals and determine how that district will set and implement strategies to achieve them.

SMART goals add clarity to vision.

The first step in setting and implementing a stretch goal is to translate it into SMART language to ensure everyone understands what it will mean to attain it. When goals are written in the SMART (Specific and Strategic, Measurable, Attainable, Results-based, and Timebound) format, stakeholders are more likely to understand what success will look like (O'Neill, 2004). This is critical because achieving a stretch goal requires the involvement of all members of a system, and the process of setting SMART goals invites involvement and establishes a process to track progress.

The SMART goal acronym can be very helpful:

- **Strategic and Specific:** Language is precise rather than vague.
- **Measurable:** The team has a clear idea of the measures it will use to assess its

progress toward the goal.

- **Attainable:** The goal is ambitious enough to demand that team members act in new ways in their classrooms, but not so ambitious that it discourages effort.

- **Results-oriented:** The goal focuses on the intended results (evidence of student learning) rather than on teacher activities such as the creation of new materials.

- **Timebound:** The team has established a timeline for the achievement of the goal (Conzemius & O'Neill, 2002, pp. 240-241).

Educators can use SMART goals to understand what the district intends to achieve and promote conversations about their role in helping. Different departments, schools, and teams may play different roles in achieving a goal. SMART educational outcomes can address the number of individuals who attain a goal, the fidelity of implementation of a program, and the date when a goal is achieved.

The attainment of SMART goals is assisted by processes to monitor progress. Measuring progress can have two important outcomes. It demonstrates that a goal is taken seriously and establishes who will be held accountable for achieving it. Secondly, visible progress can motivate individuals in their efforts to continue the hard work necessary to reach the goal. Monitoring progress toward a goal can be a visual symbol for keeping people informed of the organization's progress.

SUPPORTING EVIDENCE

The power of stretch goals.

Pasi (2003) writes, "Visionary leaders within the academic setting attempt to create cultures that will propel their schools into the future, guided by a spirit of optimism and hope. Even with all the difficulties and challenges inherent to this approach to leadership, it surely seems worth the effort" (p. 1). From the business perspective, Collins (1996) writes, "Vision is simply a combination of three basic elements: (1) an organization's fundamental reason for existence beyond just making money (often called its mission or purpose), (2) its timeless unchanging core values, and (3) huge and audacious — but ultimately achievable — aspirations for its own future" (p. 19).

Sparks (2007) writes, "Stretch goals are important because most individuals and organizations underestimate their ability to improve. … Stretch goals by their very nature require important, deep changes in the organization. Achieving stretch goals (some individuals use the 'BHAG' to prompt themselves to establish *Big Hairy Audacious Goals)* requires unrelenting focus, clarity of thought, consistent communication, alignment of resources, innovation, discipline, and teamwork" (p. 13).

Fritz and Quinn heavily influenced Sparks. Sparks (2007) wrote that Fritz believes the "structural tension" produced by the disparity between desired results and current reality precedes organizational creativity. Leaders can increase structural tension by developing a richly detailed vision of the desired results (for instance, being able to picture it as if it were being enacted in a movie or described in a press release) and by grounding discussions of current reality in data and other forms of evidence" (pp. 117-118).

"Organizations, Fritz says, resolve this tension and move forward when they act to close the gap. Fritz recommends action plans that are simple to describe and to follow. Schools then use data to assess progress (the new current reality) and design new action plans. Each creative act and the success it generates produce professional learning and energy, which breeds more creativity, learning, energy, and success" (Sparks, 2007, p. 118).

The gap between what is envisioned and the reality of what is causes a tension that produces the new and more powerful ways of thinking that are necessary to achieve the stretch goal. Sparks (2001) quotes from Robert Quinn: "Our greatest joy, no matter what our role, comes from creating. In that process, people become aware that they are able to do things they once thought were impossible. They have empowered themselves, which in turn empowers those with whom they interact" (p. 2).

The impact of accountability.

Sparks (2007) also notes: "One theory of goal setting recommends setting modest, incremental goals because people are more likely to achieve them and to experience the motivation provided by that success. This motivation, in turn, leads to continued improvement.

"Another theory says 'stretch goals' — goals so large they seem impossible to achieve — and the deep changes they require for their attainment are more valuable in producing significant, lasting improvements in schools. The benefits of both processes can be obtained when their strengths are blended. Stretch goals can stimulate deep change, while incremental 'milestone' goals can provide mid-course markers of improvement (which could be viewed as incremental goals) and offer opportunities to celebrate success and experience the motivation provided by achieving them" (p. 13).

Schmoker (1999) reinforces the importance of measuring success. "We have launched initiatives (e.g. site-based management), provided loads of staff development

in certain methods (e.g. 'Essential Elements of Instruction'), and spent untold hours drawing up visions and mission statements. All had enormous promise. But these symbolic, high-profile 'initiatives du jour' occurred in the near absence of any written or explicit intention to monitor, adjust, and thus palpably increase student learning or achievement" (p. 2).

Planning as advocated in this chapter requires discipline. Sparks (2007) observes, "Creativity of the type described here involves far more than teachers and administrators spending an hour or two writing a vision statement and brainstorming strategies. Creating schools that have at their core high levels of student and adult learning and meaningful connections among members of the school community requires the continuous development and use of professional knowledge and judgment. It also requires sustained study of professional literature, dialogue, and debate based on a candid exchange of views regarding vision, current reality, and strategies. The best way to develop these skills is by using them and by reflecting on results" (p. 119).

The Cross City Campaign for Urban School Reform (2005) made several recommendations to policy makers, practitioners, and others about creating the conditions necessary for instructional reforms to reach into schools and classrooms and contribute meaningful changes in learning and instruction:

- Superintendents need a vision of good instruction.
- Student academic needs should drive the district's policy agenda.
- Districts should be responsible for providing a plan, a realistic time line, and sufficient resources to build staff capacity when new instructional policies are adopted (p. 10).

As King and Newmann (2000) observed, "A school's instructional capacity is enhanced when its programs for student and staff learning are coherent, focused on clear learning goals, and sustained over a period of time" (p. 32). And it is the responsibility of school system leaders to assure that their planning processes produce these outcomes.

IN PRACTICE

The landmark report, *What Matters Most: Teaching for America's Future* (NCTAF, 1996) offered three assumptions about improving student learning. First, what teachers know and can do is the most important influence on what students learn. Second, recruiting, preparing, and retaining good teachers is the central strategy for improving our schools. Third, school reform cannot succeed unless it focuses on creating conditions in which teachers can teach and teach well.

To address these concerns, NCTAF challenged the nation to put a qualified teacher in every classroom. School districts that embraced the 1996 challenge invented other solutions to ensuring every child experienced high-quality teaching every day. Two strategies included sharing expertise across classrooms and among teachers, and stimulating the development of new knowledge about teaching and learning through research and studying best practice.

Over the years, several school systems began their improvement efforts with big goals, and several years later celebrated their results. In each case, a strong leader, committed to the goal, provided leadership for results. Included among these is New York City Community District 2, where Anthony Alvarado worked tirelessly to improve literacy. In Boston Public Schools, Thomas Payzant improved student achievement through a focus on teacher support. Long Beach (Calif.) Public Schools, under the leadership of Supt. Carl Cohn, celebrated a decrease in the dropout rate among 9th graders and an overall increase in high school graduation.

Rosa Smith former superintendent of the Columbus (Ohio) Public Schools, tells the story of hearing a radio report about the high percentage of young males of color who end up in jail. As she listened, her view of her work changed. She realized that "educators are not just in the reading or math or science business. We are very much in the business of saving lives" (Sparks, 2001). She remembered another statistic relating the average reading level of young black males in prisons. Teaching reading was no longer important because it offered a path to employment, teaching reading was about saving lives. Her vision for her work changed that day.

Kathy Kee, former assistant superintendent for a suburban Dallas school district, shared her BHAG at a meeting of NSDC's Board of Trustees in the mid-1990s. She had observed that her district's plan for summer school demonstrated an expectation for some students to fail. In a bold move, she eliminated funding for summer school and instead pronounced the district would no longer hold summer school for failing students. Students destined for failure would be identified earlier in the school year and served during the school year. She admitted she had no clue how to achieve her vision, just that it was incredibly important. She relied on the colleagues around her, equally moved by her goal to help chart a path. Several years later, the district had reduced summer school attendance by almost 90%. While some funds had to be allocated to summer school, had Kee never made the pronouncement the district would never have achieved its incredible results.

More than 10 years ago, Hirsh had the opportunity to spend three years working with the Corpus Christi (Texas) Independent School District to develop a comprehensive professional development plan. The process taught her valuable lessons. Most significant was the realization that the process of developing a professional development plan was actually more important than the final product because of the learning and exploration of beliefs that occurs during the development. Plans evolve from a morally compelling purpose and powerful vision for achieving audacious goals, and by determining strategic investments, and expectations for results. This process may produce a written plan, but by the time the plan is published each part is already engrained in the individuals charged with responsibility for implementation. The purpose and the vision of the work have already become the core for operational decision making, and monitoring has been integrated into the organization's work. Translating the goal into the day-to-day work of the educators responsible for achieving the goal is, in the end, what is most important.

Reeves (2006) says it another way: "The research … suggests that when it comes to planning documents, ugly beats pretty, provided that ugly is not a reflection of wanton messiness, but rather thoughtful consideration of the continuous updates and modifications that make planning documents correspond to reality. Most importantly, ugly surpasses pretty when it comes to the most important variable of all: student achievement" (p. 63). In a scathing review of the more typical planning processes adopted by school systems, Schmoker (2004) writes: "Nonetheless, these annual plans, like the hundreds I've seen since then, were approved pro forma. There was real fear of criticizing their content and so

alienating any of the numerous constituents who had spent their valuable time producing them. Instructional quality — and levels of achievement — were typically unaffected by any of these processes" (p. 425).

We propose stretch goals for students and educators. Let's begin with stretch goals for professional learning. Such stretch goals will compel the thinking and action that makes a profound difference in the practice of educators and results for students. Here are our examples of stretch goals for professional learning:

- We will eliminate all one-shot workshops.
- We will ensure all professional learning is measured against its impact on student learning.
- We will ensure every educator engages in effective professional learning every day so every student achieves.

We will begin to have new kinds of conversations regarding professional learning when school systems adopt stretch goals for students. Imagine the role of professional learning when districts adopt any of the following goals:

- All students will complete Algebra by the end of the 8th grade.
- All black males will read on grade level by the end of 3rd grade.
- All students will graduate prepared for post-secondary education, the military, or vocational training.
- All students will receive excellent teaching every day.
- Every teacher will be prepared to teach every child successfully.

CONCLUSION

Dee Hock, founder of VISA International, once said: "It is no failure to fall short of realizing all that we might dream. The failure is to fall short of dreaming all that we might realize" (1999, p. i). In our view, a key to achieving results that make a significant difference in the lives of students and educators is setting goals that make a statement about the organization's belief in the capacity of students and educators to achieve great results.

Throughout history, great leaders have relied on the motivational power of BHAGs to draw in individual creativity, commitment, and expertise to achieve what had not been previously achieved. We are convinced that if districts embraced stretch goals and the new actions called for in order to achieve them, they would produce remarkable results.

Porras, Emery, and Thompson (2007) write about another benefit of BHAGs: "They instantly capture your heart and head. They deliver clear direction. But don't confuse direction with a roadmap. …Take the race to the moon, for example. What is often forgotten is that when the BHAG of 'a man on the moon and back before the end of the decade' was conceived, America had no clue how to actually accomplish this. … It wasn't that we knew how to do it, but that we believed we had to do it" (pp. 174-175).

NSDC, too, sets big goals. The Board of Trustees in 2007 adopted the following statement as NSDC's purpose:

Every educator engages in effective professional learning every day so every student achieves.

The Board quickly translated this purpose into SMART goals by creating a 2012 timeline for achieving results that are centered around strategic priorities. The Council will call on staff, members, and all educators to engage in the kind of inventive thinking that can make such a goal a reality.

History demonstrates that setting high goals produces remarkable results. Whether the goals are those of individuals, schools, school systems, or professional associations, we believe that setting the mark high increases the potential for inventive strategies to produce the desired results.

REFERENCES

Breul, J.D. (2006). Setting stretch goals helps agencies exceed their reach. *Government Leader, 1*(9) [Electronic version]. Retrieved June 15, 2007, from www.governmentleader.com/issues/1_9/commentary/205-1.html

Collins, J. (1996). Aligning action and values. *Leader to Leader, 1*, 19-24.

Collins, J. & Porras, J.I. (2002). *Built to last.* New York: HarperCollins.

Conzemius, A. & O'Neill, J. (2002). *The handbook for SMART school teams.* Bloomington, IN: Solution Tree.

Cross City Campaign for Urban School Reform. (2005). *A delicate balance: District policies and classroom practice.* Chicago: Author.

Daley-Harris, S. (2006, November). Small steps to giant leaps: The 'micro' road out of poverty. *Vision.* Retrieved August 9, 2007, from www.vision.org/visionmedia/article.aspx?id=2028.

Hock, D. (1999). *Birth of the chaordic age.* San Francisco: Berrett-Koehler.

King, M.B. & Newmann, F.M. (2000, April). Will teacher learning advance school goals? *Phi Delta Kappan, 81*(8), 576-580.

National Commission on Teaching and America's Future. (1996). *What matters most: Teaching for America's future.* New York: Author.

O'Neill, J. (2004). Teachers learn to set goals with students. *JSD, 25*(3) 32-37.

Pasi, R. (2003). Introduction to the special issue: Leadership with vision and purpose. *NASSP Bulletin, 87*(637), 1-3.

Porras, J., Emery, S., & Thompson, M. (2007). *Success built to last: Creating a life that matters.* Upper Saddle River, NJ: Wharton School Publishing.

Reeves, D. (2006). *The learning leader: How to focus school improvement for better results.* Alexandria, VA: ASCD.

Schmoker, M. (1999). *Results: The key to continuous school improvement* (2nd ed.). Alexandria, VA: ASCD.

Schmoker, M. (2004). Tipping point: From reckless reform to substantive instructional improvement. *Phi Delta Kappan, 85*(6), 424-432.

Sparks, D. (2001). Change: It's a matter of life or slow death: An interview with Robert Quinn. *Journal of Staff Development, 22*(4), 49-53.

Sparks, D. (2001, September). Fundamental choices determine quality of professional learning. *Results,* 2.

Sparks, D. (2007). *Leading for results: Transforming teaching, learning, and relationships in schools* (2nd ed.). Thousand Oaks, CA: Corwin Press and NSDC.

Wood, C. (2002). Changing the pace of school: Slowing down the day to improve the quality of learning. *Phi Delta Kappan, 83*(7), 545-550.

"The main thing is to keep the main thing the main thing."
— *Stephen Covey*

PRINCIPLE 5

FOCUS

Maintaining the focus of professional learning
on teaching and student learning produces
academic success.

A laser is a device that emits light using a specific technology called light amplification. Unlike other sources of light such as an incandescent light bulb that emits light in almost all directions, a laser emits a narrow, well-defined beam of light that can be intense enough to cut steel.

While the scientific principles behind the construction of a laser are quite complex, the basic concept is relatively simple: Light is transmitted into a narrow pathway and is amplified as it passes through. The invention of the laser allows for the intensive concentration of light waves into a very specific space, which dramatically increases the power of the energy.

Like a laser, *focus* dramatically increases the power of the energy. Professional learning that is focused on results for students increases the impact of that learning. That focus includes concentrating on goal setting, resource allocation, effort, and evaluating professional learning in order to accomplish complex, challenging tasks more quickly and effectively.

Laser-like efforts have contributed to significant achievements in many disciplines. In the previous chapter, we discussed the contribution that stretch goals make in producing remarkable results. Yet we also recognize that stretch goals are only realized when groups focus on using powerful strategies to achieve their goals. We recall when John Kennedy challenged the nation to land a man on the moon and the excitement we felt as young students. Our teachers told us if we studied hard at math and science we would be helping our nation achieve Kennedy's goal. We recall when Martin Luther King Jr. gave his "I Have a Dream" speech and the obligations we felt to be more active in the fight for civil rights. More recently, the nation's concern has turned to the issue of global warming, and we project that most citizens can identify one or two actions they are taking to help with this crisis.

Focused effort and attention are essential to achieving great expectations. Our experience with planning has resulted in too many plans that are characterized by too many commitments, too many strategies, and too many actions. When commitments and plans become defuse, the ultimate goal is less likely to be achieved.

Schools have the capacity to accomplish bold, audacious goals related to student learning when the efforts of staff, school systems, and communities and sufficient resources are channeled through a limited number of powerful strategies. However, many professional learning and school improvement efforts lack this degree of clarity and focus. In his commissioned study for the National Governors Association, *Knowing the Right Things to Do: School Improvement and Performance-Based Accountability,* Richard Elmore concludes, "Knowing the right thing to do is the central problem of school improvement" (2003, p. 9). This committed focus is necessary to produce deep change with long-lasting results in schools that, in turn, produce success for students.

Stretch and SMART goals and expectations for achieving them provide a framework for focusing efforts. District and school leaders must be careful to avoid choosing too many paths to achieve desired outcomes. Successful plans are characterized by decisions to narrow the organization's attention to two or three powerful strategies. Following substantive research, conversation, and debate, the district and school are positioned to select strategies that are most likely to produce the results they seek. In these cases, we believe the combination of commitment and focus accelerate the organization's ability to achieve its goal.

RATIONALE

Focusing professional learning on what matters in teaching and learning ensures clarity and results. Focus requires vigilance by all educators. Each shares in the responsibility for ensuring focus on compelling goals related to teaching and learning.

"[S]chool and district leaders can provide communities with the tools and training to develop structured routines in which they systematically inquire into the relationships between their practice and the learning of their students," suggest Supovitz and Christman (2003). "Second, school and district leaders can organize data in the system so that it provides communities with meaningful information to guide their investigations. Third, they can establish processes for communities to be reviewed and provided with feedback about their instructional programs and their students' progress. Fourth, they can send a clear message throughout the system that improving instruction is the first priority of communities. Finally, they can facilitate the work of communities by helping with the logistical arrangements necessary for team teaching and cross-visitation" (p. 6).

Schmoker (1996) indicates that teachers will strengthen both their focus and practice by engaging in collaborative work. He cites Rosenholtz's research about "reciprocal relationship between goals and collegiality: Isolation 'undermines the development of shared instructional goals' (Rosenholtz, p. 17). Without clear, common goals, teachers are not able to communicate meaningfully and precisely about how to improve — and about how to determine if they are improving. Clear goals 'promote rational planning and action,' as well as 'clear criteria by which . . . performance can be evaluated' (Rosenholtz, p. 13). When clear goals are absent, schools become 'nothing more than collections of independent teachers, each marching to the step of a different pedagogical truth' (Rosenholtz, p. 17)" (Schmoker, p. 20).

One teacher leader serving as a coach to implement learning communities within a school observes:

"When one change after another keeps hitting the teachers, instead of feeling like we can really do something about improving kids' learning, the teachers start looking even more over their shoulders to find out what they're supposed to do. It's sort of a 'what's-coming-next' mentality because so much is happening" (Wood, p. 720).

In the end, many schools and districts are more like incandescent light bulbs, spreading light in all directions simultaneously. They are seduced by multiple, attractive initiatives that diffuse their energy and resources and minimize the potential for impact. Two examples stand out in the authors' experiences.

One is a small underperforming elementary school facing sanctions for poor student performance. The school received support from multiple in- and out-of-district technical assistance providers including special district programs, school-generated programs, and private and federal grant-funded programs. Within a three-year period, this small school received almost an additional $500,000 of fiscal support through 10 different programs. When an audit was conducted in the third year of low performance, the team of auditors discovered that the programs competed with one another for staff and student time and effort and had contradictory processes to achieve the goal of improving student literacy and math.

The other example is a large, urban school district whose professional development program was so fragmented that it included overlapping, competing, and repetitious programs of learning for adults. When gathered around a table to talk about their work, in-house professional development providers learned that several departments offered similar programs and replicated services. Worse, the impact of their work on student learning was missing from the conversation.

In their extensive study of the Chicago school reform program of the late 1990s, Bryk (1998) and his colleagues designated one school as the Christmas tree school. A Christmas tree school strives to compensate for deficits in student learning by bringing into the school "a plethora of programs, beautiful trade books and materials, fully-stocked labs, computers, the works" (p. 115). Both principal and teachers bring endless new ideas into the school so that school resembles "a Christmas tree laden with ornaments" (p. 115). Children are dazzled with the sparkle, yet little real learning occurs. Yet all that they tried did not add up to what they wanted most for students — improved academic outcomes, acknowledge the researchers. "The individual efforts of many different teachers and the principal had not come together to produce a collective focus on strengthening the core of the school. Their many diverse efforts remained fragmented and uncoordinated" (p. 115). They continue, "The professional staff is running itself into the ground, and the school seems likely to collapse under the burden of multiple and conflicting projects and initiatives" (p. 115). Fullan (2001) adds, "These schools glitter from a distance — so many innovations, so little time — but they end up superficially adorned with many decorations, lacking depth and coherence" (pp. 35-36).

Researchers in Chicago conclude that when a school's staff members expend tremendous effort to bring programs and services to their school, they unfortunately do not expend a concomitant amount of effort to select programs that will most closely align with existing programs and the goals for student learning in the schools. "The overall effect was a proliferation of weakly implemented and unaligned programs that might make a school look good to a casual observer," say Bryk, Sebring, Kerbow, Rollow, and Easton, "but often left staff frustrated and discouraged by the failure to realize significant improvements in student learning" (1998, p. 287).

Too often, educators can be guilty of throwing lots of interventions at challenges in hopes that one of them will be the program that helps them solve their problems. Schmoker (2002) writes: "We set goals (usually far too many), but they lack a measurable baseline. Many of them aren't goals at all. They are activities or programs (a crippling confusion in this game). Then, without even consulting the data to identify and target specific areas of underperformance, we generate and commit to a long list of action steps — an unfocused grab bag of strategies, many of them popular but unproven — that we will implement. And we have no way of knowing if or how well these actions are being implemented. We consume time and attend meetings and multi-session trainings with no plan, between meetings, to assess student performance or to adjust instruction in light of these formative results" (p. 12).

To reverse this trend of proliferation, fragmentation, and redundancy, schools and districts establish clear goals for professional learning focused on what matters, student success, so that educators engage in professional learning focused on improving instruction and student learning. Teachers and administrators can strengthen their school improvement efforts with a clear vision and compelling goals, leadership practices that provide both support and high expectations for educators and students, and teacher and leader professional learning that fosters collaboration and collective responsibility.

SUPPORTING EVIDENCE

If schools are not clear about the purpose of professional learning, any program will suffice. Too many school systems and schools can be found sightseeing as opposed to taking the interstate. Loss of focus often leads to wasteful expenditures of resources and energy. In writing about change initiatives in business, Kotter and Cohen (2002) recognize the negative effects of a lack of focus. "Far too often," they say, "guiding teams either set no clear direction or embrace visions that are not sensible. The consequences can be catastrophic for organizations and painful for employees — just ask anyone who has suffered through a useless fad focused on them from above" (p. 62).

Sparks (2007) asserts that the fundamental choices made by educational leaders are the most important factor in determining the quality of professional learning for teachers and administrators. These choices, in turn, profoundly affect their other major decisions. He cites Robert Fritz, *The Path of Least Resistance* (1989), "When people make a fundamental choice to be true to what is highest in them, or when they make a choice to fulfill a purpose in their life, they can easily accomplish many changes that seemed impossible or improbable in the past" (p. 189).

Sparks (2001) writes, "Fundamental choices are the basic orientations held by individuals about important aspects of their lives, in this case their work. These choices, in turn, determine primary choices — the major results leaders wish to create, often expressed as goals — and secondary choices — the steps taken to achieve those results, often called strategies or action plans" (p. 2).

WestEd recommends a clear focus for all improvement efforts. "It is also important to emphasize at this point the important goal of school improvement: *to improve learning opportunities for children.* With that goal kept firmly in mind, it is critical to think about the heart of the matter, the essentials. In this case, the essential aspect is instruction — the teaching-learning process. If a plan for improving a program or school is not based on a careful review of the instructional strategies being used, it is unlikely that desired outcomes will result" (Farr & Hale, 1995, p. 2).

Yet, the focus of many improvement efforts, and particularly of professional learning, continue to miss the mark. "For a long time, people focused on raising standards and writing assessments," says Sparks, "all the while forgetting about the critical element of the teacher and what transpires between a teacher and a child. As one of my colleagues put it, 'States have spent millions of dollars building the car without ever making sure we had someone who could drive it' " (2000, p. 30). "Educators and researchers have lambasted the scattered, shallow, fragmented array of activities that so often makes up the professional development landscape," says Little (2006), "reserving special criticism for activities that seem remote from teachers' priorities and problems of practice" (p. 4).

Laser-like professional learning focused on improving student learning produces deep change. Scott sums up best the critical importance of focus. "You will bring into your life whatever it is that you have the most clarity about. The trouble is, most people have a great deal of clarity about

what it is they don't want (Scott in Sparks, 2007, p. 8). Sparks (2007) adds, "Knowing what we want and being proud of it increases the likelihood we can achieve the results we seek. Intentions described in rich detail offer direction for their achievement and make it more likely we recognize valuable opportunities" (p. 8). In schools today, the focus on students often gets lost amid the many competing priorities that disburse energy, resources, and potential for results.

Corcoran, Fuhrman, and Belcher (2001) cite several reasons why school district central offices have difficulty focusing professional development that leads to improvements in teaching and learning. Among those reasons are different philosophies about the role of the district and the school in decisions about professional development; lack of evidence-based decisions and practices in favor of interests and wants, neglecting teacher content knowledge; the lack of coherence among major reform efforts, the professional development, and its providers; and multiple initiatives each with their own professional development programs contributing to a lack of focus in the district. Fuhrman and Odden (2001) conclude, "A stronger focus on instructional improvement and appropriate professional development is required for a larger payoff in student achievement" (p. 61).

Such a focus begins with clarity about student learning goals focused at the classroom and school levels. King and Newmann (2000) recognize the strong connection between a school's ability to achieve its goals and teacher learning. "A school's instructional capacity is enhanced when its programs for student and staff learning are coherent, focused on clear learning goals, and sustained over a period of time ... " (p. 578).

When the goal is student learning, the

FIGURE 1: Professional Development and the Instructional Triangle (2006)

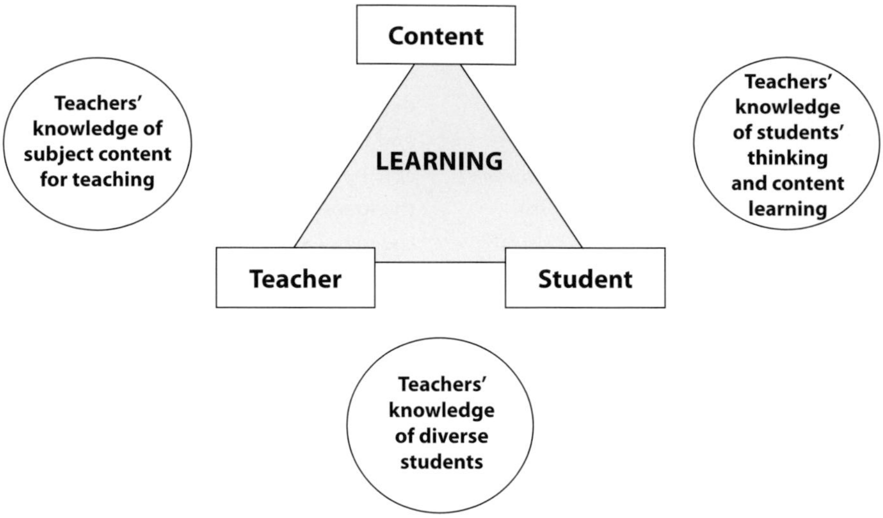

Source: Adapted from Cohen, Raudenbush, and Ball (2003).

strategies are obvious. Research by Cohen, Raudenbush, and Ball places the focus of professional learning on the instructional triangle. "The instructional triangle depicts "the relationships between teacher, students, and content. The instructional triangle encompasses the dynamic, fluid, and complex interactions by which teachers help children learn challenging subject content and pursue other important intellectual and social goals" (Little, p. 4).

The instructional triangle identifies three relationships that become the focal content for professional learning. Little describes each of these relationships. "The first is the relationship centers on teachers' understanding of subject domains for purposes of teaching" (p. 6). The second relationship is "teachers' grasp of students' thinking and learning" (p. 6). The third relationship is "teachers' understanding of and responsiveness to the students they teach, with special emphasis on understanding the nature and significance of student diversity" (p. 6).

Little cites an experimental study by Saxe, Gearhart, and Nasir (2001) that supports clearly the claim that focusing professional development on teacher content knowledge and content-specific pedagogy leads to improvement in student achievement. Researchers designed three configurations of professional development and measured changes in teaching practice and student learning. She concludes that, "The most significant effects on student learning and the most uniform shifts in teaching practice were associate with the [experimental] group having the most intensive and integrated approach to looking at mathematics, children's understanding, and assessment" (p. 7).

Focus in professional development leads to results for teachers and students. Corcoran (2007) writes: "Effective professional development is designed to help teachers meet the specific needs of real students in real classrooms" (p. 5). Focus generates clarity, overcomes resignation, builds commitment, leads to action, and produces results. With clarity of goal, educators become goal-driven and find ways to overcome obstacles. With clear goals and commitment to act, educators generate appropriate pathways to achieve identified goals.

Some schools have clear goals, just too many. In his book, *The Learning Leader*, Reeves (2006) recommends no more than six goals. "The Rule of Six, my best estimate of the maximum number of priorities on which a leader could focus, noting that those who claimed to have dozens of 'priorities,' in fact, had none. Because every leader has far more than a half dozen people, tasks, projects, and constituencies all clamoring for priority treatment, the task of the systems leader is to know which of those competing factors have the greatest leverage" (pp. 46-47).

With clarity of goals, commitment to act, and designated pathways, leaders are more able to allocate appropriate effort and resources to accomplish the goals. With clarity of goals, motivation to act, clear pathways, and appropriate resources, educators are more likely to achieve their goals. With clear goals, commitment, pathways, and resources, professional learning then targets educators' knowledge, attitudes, skills, aspirations, and behaviors to ensure student learning. Three different examples of how tightly focused efforts aligned with specific goals for students achieve results follow.

IN PRACTICE

Boston Public School's Collaborative Literacy program offers an example of how focus improved results. When BPS initiated instructional coaching in literacy in 2002, the services of coaches were available on a volunteer basis. When results were not as dramatic as hoped, the district revamped the coaching efforts to be focused, multi-week intensive support to a team of teachers. The transition resulted in significant changes in classroom literacy instruction and student learning (Schwartz & McCarthy, 2003).

Pittsburgh Public Schools found that schools can close the achievement gap if reform efforts tightly align curriculum, assessment, instruction, and professional development to high-quality content (Lewis, 2001).

Researchers in the Bay Area School Reform Collaborative discovered that achievement gaps between black and Hispanic students, and white and Asian students disappear when teachers analyze data about student learning and diagnose students' learning needs frequently, and use that information to target instruction (Asimov, 2003). Analyzing data enables teachers to understand student learning needs more clearly and therefore be able to address those needs through classroom instruction. When teachers know how to determine the gaps in student learning, they use laser-like focus in teaching to address those gaps so students progress toward rigorous, content-specific standards.

Too often, school systems, in an attempt to establish common direction and goals for the system fail to identify the specific needs of students and their teachers. When this process is reversed to use backwards planning models for professional learning such as those recommended by Killion (2002) and Guskey (2000, 2001), the primary purpose of learning for adults is learning for students. Students will benefit when student learning needs are the focus for educators' professional learning and the entire educational system aligns to support both students and educators. Beginning

FIGURE 2: Nested System of Supports for Learning

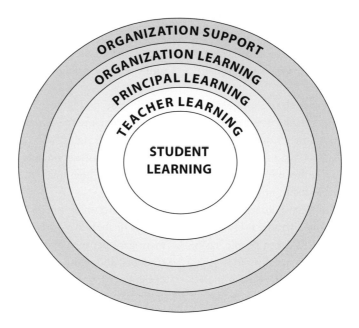

with the larger system efforts and hoping that those efforts trickle down to the classroom may lead to more sightseeing and fewer results.

Figure 2 provides one example of the nested system that supports learning for students.

Focusing professional learning on what matters in the classroom is the responsibility of all stakeholders throughout the educational system. In *Moving NSDC's Standards Into Practice: Innovation Configurations*, Roy, Hord, and Hirsh (2003, 2005) recognize the importance of 10 distinct different stakeholder groups that share responsibility for professional learning that improves the learning of all students. Killion and Harrison (2006) identify the 11th role of school-based staff developers. According to Little (2006), "school leaders would support teachers in acquiring deep understanding of what it means for children to learn core

concepts and skills in particular subject domains. School staff would develop the habit of collectively examining evidence of student learning and investigating the sources of students' progress or difficulties. Teachers would be helped to locate and participate in the best of external professional development opportunities and to parlay what they learned into collective capacity in the school. Partnerships with organizations or groups outside the school would be strategically chosen for their contribution to professional development and professional community" (pp. 4, 6).

The central office also has a responsibility to create and sustain professional learning focused on improving teaching and leading practices and student learning. Fuhrman and Odden (2001), reporting on the work of Corcoran, Fuhrman, and Belcher, suggest that, "Central office staff members want to adopt best practices, but they lack coherent strategies for making evidence-based decisions, and most districts struggle with creating adequate internal supports and maintaining a consistent focus," they state. "In addition, districts significantly under invest in appropriate professional development" (p. 6).

Educators might consider the advantage of developing a personal theory of change. Establishing a theory of change offers the best chance for the strategies to produce the desired outcome and prevent the system from over investing in multiple strategies that may not produce better results and could dissipate the impact of those strategies with the most potential to produce the desired outcomes. Killion (2002) writes that a theory of change "…delineates the underlying assumptions upon which the program is based. It includes not only the components of a program, but also incorporates an explanation of how the change is expected to occur" (p. 55). Asking the team to clarify its theory of change — how the action plan will produce the results it seeks — and discussing the assumptions team members hold about that process increase the likelihood that the plan will achieve its goals.

Effective school leaders realize that knowing what not to do is as important as knowing what to do. Reeves (2006) describes these phenomena and recommends that leaders learn to focus their attention on teaching and leadership practices that are most often associated with positive student results. In his Leadership for Learning Framework, Reeves offers a way to explore teaching and leadership practices in order to distinguish those that are important areas of focus. About leadership, he says, "Leaders are plagued by expectations that are out of line with reality. … When leaders shift their focus from large numbers of random practices with random effects to a small number of intersections … they nurture, support, and recognize their most effective hubs, and break the toxic connections stemming from the most poisonous hubs" (p. 167). Reeves continues, "Focused leaders engage in daily disciplines that maximize their energy, bringing the highest level of concentrated effort on the challenges that are most important" (pp. 167-168).

"To build a culture that focuses on results, schools can say, 'No!' Effective school leaders are a buffer between staff and those well-intentioned souls (legislators, governors, reformers, central office, parents, etc.) who want to press their agendas on the schools," posit DuFour and Burnette (2002). "They recognize that the world's capacity to generate ideas to improve schools exceeds the staff's capacity to implement meaningful change. Thus they work with staff to clarify a shared vision of the school they are trying to create. They identify a few initiatives that offer the greatest leverage for moving the school in that direction. Most importantly, they focus collective efforts and energies on those few initiatives and resist the temptation to pursue other worthwhile projects" (p. 29).

Teachers also have a responsibility to maintain focus in their professional learning. This effort grows exponentially if teachers work collaboratively. All stakeholders are responsible for seeking and maintaining focus. Together, they keep at bay the seductive distractions that diffuse resources and effort. They make all decisions through a filter that sorts out what does not contribute to student learning. They ask themselves frequently, Whose interests are being served by this decision or action? If the answer is not "students," they return to the table to revamp their actions.

CONCLUSION

John F. Kennedy's words and the subsequent landing of Neil Armstrong and Buzz Aldrin on the moon are an example of a laser-focused effort in which all effort and resources support a single, audacious goal.

"Now it is time to take longer strides — time for a great new American enterprise — time for this nation to take a clearly leading role in space achievement, which in many ways may hold the key to our future. … I believe we possess all the resources and all the talents necessary. But the facts of the matter are that we have never made the national decisions or marshaled the national resources required for such leadership. We have never specified long-range goals on an urgent time schedule, or managed our resources and our time so as to ensure their fulfillment," said Kennedy (1961).

Kennedy's words are as relevant today as they were nearly 50 years ago. The nation must muster its collective wisdom on improving learning for every student by recognizing that learning for all educators is the single most important pathway for improving student learning. If Kennedy's plea for a high level of commitment to the profoundly challenging goal of reaching the moon were replaced today with the goal of ensuring that every educator engages in daily collaborative learning to ensure that all students learn, the message is more than fitting.

REFERENCES

Asimov, N. (2003, December 18). Testament to testing: Schools close 'achievement gap' by pinpointing trouble spots worth frequent assessments. *San Francisco Chronicle*, A21.

Bryk, A., Sebring, P., Kerbnow, D., Rollow, S., & Easton, J. (1998). *Charting Chicago school reform: Democratic localism as a lever for change*. Boulder, CO: Westview Press.

Corcoran, T. (2007). Teaching matters: How state and local policymakers can improve the quality of teachers and teaching. *CPRE Policy Briefs*, RB 48.

Corcoran, T., Furhman, S., & Belcher, C. (2001). The district role in instructional improvement. *Phi Delta Kappan, 83*(1), 78-84.

DuFour, R. & Burnette, B. (2002). Pull out negativity by its roots. *Journal of Staff Development, 23*(3), 27-30.

Elmore, R. (2003). *Knowing the right thing to do: School improvement and performance-based accountability.* Washington, DC: National Governors Association Center for Best Practices.

Farr, B. & van Heusden Hale, S. (1995). *Focus on school improvement: A planning guide.* San Francisco: WestEd.

Fritz, R. (1989). *The path of least resistance: Learning to become the creative force in your own life.* New York: Fawcett.

Fuhrman, S. & Odden, A. (2001). Redefining government roles in an era of standards-based reform. *Phi Delta Kappan, 83*(1), 59-61.

Fullan, M. (2001). *Leading in a culture of change.* San Francisco: Jossey-Bass.

Guskey, T. (2000). *Evaluating professional development.* Thousand Oaks, CA: Corwin Press.

Guskey, T. (2001). The backward approach. *Journal of Staff Development, 22*(3), 60.

Hord, S., Hirsh, S., & Roy, P. (2005). *Moving NSDC's standards into practice: Innovation configurations, Volume II.* Oxford, OH: NSDC.

Kennedy, J.F. (1961, May 25). Urgent national needs. Speech to the Joint Session of Congress. Presidential Files, John F. Kennedy Library. Boston.

www.jfklibrary.org/Historical+Resources/
Archives/Reference+Desk/Speeches/JFK/
03POF03NationalNeeds05251961.htm.
Downloaded March 6, 2007.

Killion, J. (2002). *Assessing impact: Evaluating staff development.* Oxford, OH: NSDC.

Killion, J. & Harrison, C. (2006). *Taking the lead: New roles for teachers and school-based coaches.* Oxford, OH: NSDC.

King, M.B. & Newmann, F.M. (2000). Will teacher learning advance school goals? *Phi Delta Kappan, 81*(8), 576-580.

Kotter, J. & Cohen D. (2002). *The heart of change: Real-life stories of how people change their organizations.* Boston: Harvard Business School Press.

Lewis, A.C. (2001). A performance test for districts and states. *Phi Delta Kappan, 82*(8), 567-568.

Little, J.W. (2006). *Professional community and professional development in the learning-centered school.* Washington, DC: National Education Association.

Reeves, D. (2006). *The learning leader: How to focus school improvement for better results.* Alexandria, VA: ASCD.

Roy, P. & Hord, S. (2003). *Moving NSDC's standards into practice: Innovation configurations, Volume I.* Oxford, OH: NSDC.

Saxe, G.B., Gearhart, M., & Nasir, N. (2001). Enhancing students' understanding of mathematics: A study of three contrasting approaches to professional support. *Journal of Mathematics Teacher Education, 4*(1), 55-79.

Schmoker, M. (1996). *Results: the key to continuous school improvement.* Alexandria, VA: ASCD.

Schmoker, M. (2001). *The results fieldbook: Practical strategies from dramatically improved schools.* Alexandria, VA: ASCD.

Schmoker, M. (2002). Up and away. *Journal of Staff Development, 23*(2), 10-13.

Schwartz, S. & McCarthy, M. (2003). *Where the rubber hits the road: An in-depth look at Collaborative Coaching and Learning and workshop instruction in a sample of Effective Practice Schools.* Boston: Boston Plan for Excellence.

Sparks, D. (2000). It all comes down to the teacher: An interview with Terry Dozier. *Journal of Staff Development, 21*(4), 30-33.

Sparks, D. (2001, September). Fundamental choices determine quality of professional learning. *Results, 2.*

Sparks, D. (2007). *Leading for results: Transforming teaching, learning, and relationships in schools* (2nd ed.). Thousand Oaks, CA: Corwin Press and NSDC.

Supovitz, J.A. & Christman, J.B. (2003). Developing communities of instructional practice: Lessons from Cincinnati and Philadelphia. *CPRE Policy Briefs,* RB-39.

Wood, C. (2002). Changing the pace of school: Slowing down the day to improve the quality of learning. *Phi Delta Kappan, 83*(7), 545-550.

"Everything that can be counted does not necessarily count; everything that counts cannot necessarily be counted."
— *Albert Einstein*

IMPACT

Evaluation strengthens performance and results.

In December 1997, Hayes Mizell, now NSDC's Distinguished Senior Fellow, delivered a stinging message to those gathered at NSDC's annual conference in Nashville, Tenn. Some in the audience remarked that the message sounded like an accusation or rebuke and resented it. Mizell called upon his listeners to take up the challenge of finding programs of educator learning that focus on deepening teachers' content knowledge and content-specific pedagogy and then finding the evidence that staff development impacts student learning.

"The need for effective evaluation of staff development is illustrated by the expectations of those who conceive staff development and those who participate in it. Judging from the nature of much staff development, a reasonable person might ask, 'Did the people responsible for this really expect it to have much effect on the participants?' If so, it seems they would have conceived the staff development activity very differently, devoted greater care to involving representatives of the potential audience in its planning, and invested as much effort planning what would happen after the staff development as in the staff development itself. They certainly would have conceived staff development with the intention to have a direct effect on student learning, and, from the beginning, clearly communicated that intent to the participants. ... Is it important enough to evaluate its effects? Does staff development really make a difference, and how do you know? Evaluation is the Achilles' heel of staff development. ... In this context, where expectations about results are so low among those who conceive and plan staff development and those who participate in it, the absence of rigorous evaluation only aggravates the problem. If no one is asking hard questions there is no incentive for the expectations to change. I question whether staff development will ever have the impact I believe it should unless school systems and schools, as well as researchers, become much more serious about evaluating its effects on the performance of teachers, administrators, and students. This evaluation will be difficult, but those who believe staff development is important have to try. . . . The challenges to staff development are huge, and it is an open question whether it is up to the task. As it currently exists in most schools and school systems, there is little reason to be encouraged" (Mizell, 1997).

Indeed, it was a moment of transformation. Mizell's speech marked a turning point at NSDC and in the field. His challenge has led NSDC and others to concentrate efforts on engaging teachers in the professional learning experiences that would most impact student achievement and on evaluating the impact in order to improve practice and demonstrate results. NSDC took up the gauntlet Mizell threw down that day and launched two initiatives. One was the *Results-based Staff Development Initiative,* funded by the Edna McConnell Clark Foundation and the National Education Association. The second was *Demonstrating the Impact,* also funded by the Clark Foundation. Both initiatives moved the field of professional learning into the results-based era.

The statement, "what gets measured, gets done," surfaces in many discussions about evaluation. The statement has a number of assumptions embedded in it. First among them is that what gets done is elevated to a higher level of importance or urgency if it has evaluation associated with it. Second, evaluation is a great motivator to accomplish the established goals. Third, the pressure of evaluation can encourage action.

We believe that evaluation goes beyond getting things done to getting things done

well and to producing the desired results. The principle is this: Evaluation strengthens performance and results. In *Assessing Impact: Evaluating Staff Development* (2002), Killion notes that "results-oriented leaders know how to create systems, build coalitions, motivate employees, monitor performance for effectiveness, and be responsible for results. Osborne and Gaebler (1992) remind us that results-oriented leaders live by these principles:

- What gets measured gets done.
- If results are not measured, it will be difficult to distinguish success from failure.
- If success is not visible, it will be difficult to measure it.
- If success can't be rewarded, then failure probably is.
- If success isn't visible, it is difficult to learn from it.
- If failure is not recognized, it is difficult to correct it.
- If results are demonstrated, public support follows (p. 127).

The purpose of evaluation is to judge the merit, worth, and/or impact of a set of actions, resources, interventions, etc. Evaluation carries weight. Sometimes, the weight of evaluation is oppressive and debilitating, often evoking fear of monitoring and accountability. Other times, evaluation is motivational and compelling, urging those engaged to reach for ambitious goals. Evaluation carries weight in the design of professional development as well. If professional development is not carefully planned and sufficient in its design, then professional development cannot produce the desired results.

In the field of professional development, what is being measured is the composite of professional learning experiences. Evaluation provides information not only about the impact of professional learning on leading, teaching, and student learning, but also about the strengths and weaknesses of its processes. The results can guide design and implementation of future professional learning efforts.

APQC, an international benchmarking organization, presents an additional value of evaluating professional development. "We would add one more purpose: In the face of ever-shrinking budgets, quantifiable evaluation data is needed so policy makers and district leadership can sustain the needed resources to support a quality learning environment for staff and students" (2007, p. 67). Assessing the impact of professional learning requires careful planning of both the professional development and the evaluation methodology. This process strengthens the design of professional learning as well as the evaluation. If we intend to evaluate, we are more likely to simultaneously intend to achieve results. With this intention, we plan sufficient and powerful strategies to achieve those results.

RATIONALE

We evaluate to improve both performance and results. "Evaluation is important," says Mizell (2003), "because if educators are going to get the staff development they need to help their students perform proficiently, they will have to demonstrate that adult learning can significantly increase student achievement. The field of staff development needs better evaluation both to improve the effectiveness of teachers' learning experiences and to produce credible evidence that will garner more support for professional development" (p. 12). Evaluation ensures that improvements or adjustments are driven by carefully analyzed evidence. Because the purpose of evaluation of professional development is to assess its

worth, merit, and impact, we gain information to use as a basis for decisions about changes we make. "Only by using a sensible and sensitive approach to evaluation will we be able to know what is working, what is not, and what to change, as well as what to keep," assert Kaufman, Guerra, and Platt (2006). "We can do educational evaluation to create a positive and productive learning environment that delivers worthy results and avoids the wrong things. We want evaluation data that lead to good decisions. As professionals, we know that good evaluation helps us take responsibility for what we do and for the consequences of our actions" (p. vii).

When evaluating professional learning, we want to know if it works, how it works, and what changes it produces. We seek to identify areas for improvement to strengthen professional learning and its application. We commit to continuous improvement. The basic questions that drive evaluation are:

- What's working? How do we know?
- What isn't working? How do we know?
- What will we do to improve what we are doing to produce even better results? (Killion, 2002).

Guskey (2000) recognizes that accountability is one of the factors driving the increase in interest in the evaluation of staff development. But he cites three other reasons as well:

- A better understanding of the "dynamic nature" of professional development.
- Recognition of professional development as "an intentional process."
- The need for better information to guide reform efforts (p. 8).

Although evaluation evokes in some the fear of accountability, Guskey (2000) provides a more positive perspective: "Some individuals in education see this emphasis on accountability and, hence, evaluation as detrimental to our progress. They fear that it presents undue pressure for evidence that will diminish the roles of artistry, clinical judgment, and reflection in educational work. But this need not be so. Just as is true in other professions such as medicine or engineering, improved understanding of the processes and procedures that lead to success allow the artistry, judgment, and reflection to become more valid and effective in reaching our ideals (Gage, 1997). Well-designed evaluations do the same. They enrich our understanding of professional development processes and procedures and thereby allow the dimensions of artistry, judgment, and reflection to become all the more meaningful because they are based on evidence of success" (p. 8).

Elmore (2002) notes: "Schools, as organizations, aren't designed as places where people are expected to engage in sustained improvement of their practice, where they are supported in this improvement, or where they are expected to subject their practice to the scrutiny of peers or the discipline of evaluation based on student achievement" (p. 1). Improving performance and results, however, requires evaluation.

Evaluation provides the essential information that allows decision makers to know if the efforts are worthwhile, if they produce intended results, and if they can be improved. Evaluation — not just data — is increasingly important for improving professional development and its results. Evaluation provides a way for school and district leaders to answer questions about the impact of professional development, determine funding priorities, strengthen and focus their professional development efforts, and improve teaching and student learning.

SUPPORTING EVIDENCE

Evaluation has two overarching benefits. First, evaluation, if well designed, provides evidence to measure progress toward and achievement of goals. Knowing if we have achieved our goals will be difficult unless we have evidence of the accomplishment. Second, evaluation provides information that is essential to improve quality of our efforts in achieving results. When we improve quality, we simultaneously improve results. The cyclical nature of evaluation-improvement-evaluation-improvement is fundamental to many quality practices.

In a study of nine high schools selected for their evidence of continuous improvement practices, Ingram, Seashore-Louis, and Schroeder (2002) found that even when the school is committed to continuous improvement using data-driven decision making, cultural, political, and technical challenges prevent both teachers as individuals or schools as collective communities from engaging in routine evaluation practices designed to promote data-based decisions about school improvements.

In a succinct statement, Hatry states, "Unless you are keeping score, it is difficult to know whether you are winning or losing" (p. 1). Osborne and Gaebler add, "If you don't measure results, you can't tell success from failure" (p. 147). Leaders know the importance of measuring progress toward a goal and making adjustments along the way to increase the likelihood of achieving the goal.

Cicchinelli and Camarena (1999) advocate that evaluations that produce useful information should not be afterthoughts, but should be part of program planning and implementation from the onset. Evaluation without thoughtful and thorough planning for success in professional development is inexcusable, says Killion (2002). Consequently, the evaluation process begins with planning powerful professional learning experiences integrated into a coordinated program that will ensure deep understanding of key concepts, skills to implement the understanding, and ongoing opportunities for support, reflection, and refinement, along with continuous examination of progress and impact (Killion, 2002).

In reflecting on the eight forces leaders use to prevent failure in reform efforts, Fullan, Cuttress, and Kilcher (2005) call for cultures of evaluation. "Cultures of evaluation serve external accountability and internal data processing," they say. "They produce data on an ongoing basis that enable groups to use information for action planning as well as for external accounting" (p. 56). They continue, "When schools and school systems increase their collective capacity to engage in ongoing assessment for learning, they achieve major improvements" (p. 56).

A part of the process of measuring progress toward a set of goals and even the process for determining a course of action is understanding clearly where the organization currently is in relationship to the goals it wishes to achieve. "All good-to-great companies," according to Collins (2001), "began the process of finding a path to greatness by confronting the brutal facts of their current reality" (p. 88).

Conducting evaluation alone is insufficient. Patton (1997) stresses the gap between knowledge and use of knowledge as a pitfall of evaluation. He advocates for "narrowing the gap between generating evaluation findings and actually using those findings for program decision making and improvement. ... The issue of use has emerged at the interface between science and action, between knowing and doing. It raises fundamental questions about human

rationality, decision making, and knowledge applied to creation of a better world" (p. 4). The real value of evaluation lies not only in knowing if results were achieved, but also in understanding how they were achieved.

IN PRACTICE

To turn evaluation from a fear-evoking process to one viewed as a natural part of continuous improvement, two essential factors are needed. One is a culture in which people are comfortable describing success and struggles and the second is the willingness to brutally examine the truth. The process of confronting current reality and of evaluating efforts to improve it occurs best in a climate where truth is heard and where people have access to information, according to Jim Collins (2001). He recommends four techniques leaders can use to engage people in these processes.

- **Lead with questions, not answers.**

  Leaders ask questions to understand, seek answers from others rather than giving answers, and engage small groups of individuals in informal meetings with no agenda other than asking questions like: " 'So what's on your mind?' 'Can you tell me about that?' 'Can you help me understand?' 'What should we be worried about?' " (p. 75).

- **Engage in dialogue and debate, not coercion.**

  Leaders engage others in honest, open communication about what is possible, what makes sense, and what to do. Sometimes, these conversations deteriorate into debates and arguments but those engaged share a common desire to achieve positive results and that unifying goal keeps the focus on the work and not individuals.

- **Conduct autopsies without blame.**

  Spending time understanding and learning from situations that go awry rather than finding who is to blame produces useful information for improvements.

- **Build red flag mechanisms.**

Waving a red flag is a symbolic way for people to make observations, voice their opinions, state their assumptions, make a suggestion, or ask a question. When leaders encourage people to share in this way they have access to useful and valuable information to identify potential problems and make improvements.

The Florida Department of Education's Professional Development System Evaluation Protocol requires every Florida school district to demonstrate competence in four broad standards for professional development, one of which is evaluation. The initial school district reviews revealed that districts struggled with evaluation of professional development. The Tri-County Collaborative comprising Miami-Dade County, Palm Beach County, and Broward County decided to change that. Working together across school system lines, the district leaders in staff development gathered everyone responsible for providing professional development to teach them about the new state standards for professional development and to engage them in a two-year learning experience about evaluating their efforts and to apply their learning to the professional development they managed. They met three days a year for two years to learn about evaluation and evaluation strategies, to design and conduct evaluations, and to engage in peer review of their work. As a result of their collaborative work, the districts have a renewed investment in quality evaluation and are implementing processes to ensure ongoing evaluation of their professional development programs.

In fall 2006, 27 school districts from throughout North America participated in a benchmarking study of their professional development programs. Districts volunteered to complete interviews and an extensive survey in order to compare their professional development programs to identified best-practices districts. One of the major findings of this study was the need to invest more time and effort in evaluating the impact of professional development. Districts discovered that they lacked the knowledge base, skill level, and technology to determine the impact of their professional development on student learning, something they all wanted to do (Killion & Colton, 2007). As a result, APQC, the benchmarking organization responsible for conducting the study, launched a new study in fall 2007 focused exclusively on the evaluation of professional development.

In schools, data discussions offer profound learning experiences for all educators. In these powerful conversations, teachers and others strive to make sense of a wide range of data. They identify patterns from their observations, work to identify probable root causes, and plan improvement efforts. Data conversations, says Killion (2002), give educators the opportunity to "gain an understanding of the need for change, establish priorities, take responsibility for their actions, and tell each other the truth about their work. Energy, commitment, and focus emerge from these conversations" (p. 125).

Yet data conversations are not evaluation, but rather a part of the evaluation process. To turn data analysis into evaluation, an evaluation framework or plan is necessary. "An evaluation framework creates a rigorous, systematic, and purposeful approach to data gathering, analysis, and interpretation. The evaluation framework begins with posing questions that stakeholders want to answer. The framework guides their work and focuses attention on the proximal factors — those most directly in the school's control — and keeps attention away from the distal factors — those over which schools have very little control. An evaluation framework makes the work of data analysis results-focused, not process-focused" (Killion, 2002, p. 125).

To strengthen their evaluation processes, educators can move from collecting data to using data to make improvement. "Data alone are not useful unless they are placed within the context of a systematic investigation of programs and processes. Evaluation — not just data — is becoming increasingly important for reforming schools" (Killion, 2002, p. 125). This is precisely what the teachers and principal at Creekside Elementary School in Stockton, Calif. did. They used data about student learning to question the effectiveness of their own practices in teaching writing. Working with consultant Linda Munger, the school's principal and staff became better informed about teaching writing. Student writing was assessed three times during the school year. As grade-level teams, the teachers scored student writing samples using the district writing rubrics and then differentiated their teaching practices and student writing assignments based on the student results. Teachers also worked with the district literacy coach and later school-based writing coaches to support their learning and application to impact student writing. As a result, student writing performance has continually increased.

In Indiana, PL221 requires schools to identify the new knowledge, skills, and attitudes toward learning that will result from professional development. The principal and teachers at Garden City Elementary School in the Metropolitan School District of Wayne Township in Indianapolis, Ind., became more engaged in "evaluation think," which helped focus their collection of data

regarding the school's progress toward achieving its goal of increasing student achievement in reading comprehension. Grade-level teams and the building professional development team examined on a regular basis teacher implementation (e.g. grade-level team logs, classroom observation data, implementation logs, and student work samples) to design professional development based on teacher evidence and student data to determine what was and was not impacting student achievement. As a result of this collective focus on assessing teacher effectiveness and student improvement in reading comprehension, student achievement scores as measured on the statewide assessment for English and language arts for the 2006-07 school year increased beyond the school improvement goal of 70% set for all grades.

Collins (2001) called this use of data a distinguishing feature between good-to-great companies and comparison companies. "Indeed, we found no evidence that the good-to-great companies had more or better information than their comparison companies. None. Both sets of companies had virtually identical access to good information. The key then lies not in better information, but in turning information into information that *cannot be ignored*" (p. 79).

Some evaluations of professional learning, according to Guskey (2000), are shallow. They fail to provide evidence about the worth, merit, and impact of professional development. *Worth* is the perception of value of the professional development experience to those participating. Questions associated with *worth* are: Did I enjoy the program? Did it have value to me? Were the time and effort I invested worthwhile to me in terms of the benefits I received? Yet evaluations of worth alone will do little to satisfy the hunger of policy makers and decision makers for meaningful and substantial information to guide decisions regarding the program.

To be able to provide this type of information, evaluation must minimally provide evidence about whether the program achieved its goals. *Merit* is the degree to which the professional development met the established goals. Questions associated with *merit* are: Did the program achieve its goals? Which goals did it achieve? Which goals did it not achieve? However, if those goals are service-oriented rather than results-oriented, it will be important to look at impact. What changed as a result of the program and how did those changes occur?

Impact refers to the changes associated with professional development. Questions associated with impact are: What changed in my teaching practices as a result of what I learned? What do I know now that I didn't know before? What changed for my students? What changed in the school's culture?

Evaluations that produce information on the impact of professional development provide information for improving a program. They require a commitment of both time and resources: Time to allow the program to take effect and time to design data collection methods that are naturally embedded rather than burdensome, and to gather and analyze the data and resources to support the program's full implementation.

Evaluation of new forms of professional learning that extend beyond the training or workshop model of learning pose new challenges to those ready to evaluate them. Today's professional learning is more collaborative in nature, situated in teams rather than whole districts or schools, is focused on the work of the educators within the team and their classrooms, and occurs daily and informally. This presents added challenges to evaluators. "In and of themselves, the newer types of staff development mean little," notes Mizell (2003). "What matters is the degree to which they cause educators to develop and apply practical knowledge and skills that increase student achievement. It will require more intentional, consistent, and robust evaluations to determine whether and how neo-professional development is more powerful than its predecessor" (p. 12).

However, educators can evaluate this new system of professional development by using Kirkpatrick's (1998) four levels of training evaluation — participant response to the learning, participant learning, participant application of learning, and results for the client — plus Guskey's (2000) added level of organizational change.

An evaluation of the impact of team-based professional learning, for example, would seek evidence to answer questions such as these:

- **Worth:**
  o Do team members value their collaborative time?
  o What do they value about their collaborative time?
  o What benefits do learning team members identify?
- **Merit:**
  o Do learning teams set goals based on student achievement data?
  o Are those goals achieved?
  o How have the interventions that have been selected and planned by the team impacted the results?
  o How cohesive is the learning team?
- **Impact:**
  o What changes in teaching practice occurred as a result of members' changed teaching practices?
  o How has student learning changed as a result of changes in teaching practices?
  o How has the whole school culture changed as a result of the use of learning teams?

o   What professional collaboration skills did members gain?

- **Processes:**

o   How are those goals achieved?

o   How have the teams selected and planned interventions impacted the results they produced?

o   How do learning team members overcome problems associated with interpersonal relationships?

o   What processes do team members use within their team meetings?

o   How do team members use their team time?

o   What challenges do teams face?

With the answers to these questions and evidence to support them, schools or districts can make decisions about continuing to support collaborative learning teams, whether to provide more or fewer resources, what knowledge and skill development is necessary to improve the work of collaborative learning teams, and whether collaborative learning teams produce the results intended. Evaluation framed around these questions will provide the evidence to both improve the performance of learning teams as well as their results.

CONCLUSION

Evaluation strengthens performance and results. Those committed to continuous improvement will undertake the important work of evaluation. Yet too many educators, as Collins (2005) says about those in social sectors, throw up their hands and say that measuring performance in social sectors such as education in the same way as business is impossible. He suggests that it is "simply lack of discipline." In education, too many confuse research with evaluation and set unrealistic expectations for the evaluations they conduct. Collins reminds us that "all indicators are flawed, whether

qualitative or quantitative. . . . What matters is not finding the perfect indicator, but settling upon a *consistent and intelligent* method of assessing your output results, and then tracking your trajectory with rigor" (p. 8). Collins continues, "Any journey from good to great requires relentlessly adhering to these input variables, rigorously tracking your trajectory on the output variables, and then driving yourself to even higher levels of performance and impact. No matter how much you have achieved, *you will always be merely good relative to what you can become*" (p. 9). He adds, "It doesn't really matter whether you can quantify your results. What matters is that you rigorously assemble evidence — quantitative or qualitative — to track your progress" (p. 7).

We must be thinking more rigorously, realistically, and precisely about why we do what we do, what ends we hope to accomplish, and how we can document our successes in achieving those ends, proposes Schorr (2000). Mizell's comments in 1997 began a significant turn in the evaluation practices in schools and school systems.

"Getting serious about evaluating professional development demonstrates that a school system or school is truly serious about improving teacher and student performance" (Mizell, 2003, p. 13). We believe that in the next decade the challenge of evaluating professional learning will be resolved through collaborative efforts among educators who want to know if their learning processes are making a difference in leading, teaching, and student learning.

REFERENCES

APQC. (2007). *Professional development final report.* Houston, TX: Author.

Cicchinelli, L. & Camarena, M. (1999). Evaluating comprehensive school reform initiatives. In *Noteworthy perspectives* *on comprehensive school reform* (pp. 41-48). Aurora, CO: Mid-Continent Regional Educational Laboratory.

Collins, J. (2001). *Good to great: Why some companies make the leap …and others don't.* New York: HarperCollins.

Collins, J. (2005). *Good to great and the social sectors: A monograph to accompany good to great.* Boulder, CO: Author.

Elmore, R. (2002, November). Want to improve schools? Invest in the people who work in them. *Results*, 1.

Fullan, M., Cuttress, C., & Kilcher, A. (2005). Eight forces for leaders of change. *JSD, 24*(4), 54-64.

Guskey, T. (2000). *Evaluating professional development.* Thousand Oaks, CA: Corwin Press.

Hatry, H. (1978). The status of productivity measurement in the public sector. *Public Administration Review 38*(1), 28-33.

Ingram, D., Seashore-Louis, K., & Schroeder, L. (2004). Accountability policies and teacher decision making: Barriers to the use of data to improve practice. *Teachers College Record, 106*(6), 1258-1287.

Kaufman, R., Guerra, I., & Platt, W. (2006). *Practical evaluation for educators.*

Thousand Oaks, CA: Corwin Press.

Killion, J. (2002). *Assessing impact: Evaluating staff development.* Oxford, OH: NSDC.

Killion, J. & Colton, T. (2007). *Professional development benchmarking consortia study.* www.nsdc.org/library/APQC-NSDC. pdf.

Kirkpatrick, D. (1998). *Evaluating training: The four levels* (2nd ed.). San Francisco: Berrett-Koehler.

Mizell, H. (2003). Facilitator 10, refreshments 8, evaluation 0. *JSD, 24*(4), 10.

Mizell, H. (1997, December 9). *Is staff development a smart investment?* Speech given at NSDC Annual Conference, Nashville, TN. www.middleweb.com/ HMNSDC2.html

Osborne, D. & Gaebler, T. (1992). *Reinventing government: how the entrepreneurial spirit is transforming the public sector.* Reading, MA: Addison-Wesley.

Patton, M.Q. (1997). *Utilization-focused evaluation* (3rd ed.). Thousand Oaks, CA: Sage Publications.

Schorr, L. (2000, July 12). The intersection of school and community, *Education Week, 19*, 42.

"Never become so much of an expert that you stop gaining expertise. View life as a continuous learning experience."
— Denis Waitley

EXPERTISE

Communities can solve even their most complex problems by tapping internal expertise.

When teachers work collaboratively, build on one another's experiences, and use those experiences as a source of learning, they have the potential to meet nearly every challenge they face related to teaching and learning. By sharing teacher expertise in communities of practice, teachers develop a stronger sense of collective responsibility for their own practices and those of their colleagues. "Teacher expertise," according to York-Barr and Duke (2004), "is at the foundation of increasing teacher quality and advancements in teaching and learning" (p. 258). Shared expertise is the driver of instructional change, according to Elmore and Burney (1997). Knowledge sharing and construction is the hallmark of 21st-century educators, acknowledges Fullan (2001). When expertise is shared, solutions to complex problems emerge from within the community.

Teacher expertise emanates from many sources including preparation and experience. However, it is the learning in and from practice that cements expertise. Honing teachers' expertise rather than focusing on their knowledge, skills, years of experience, preparation, or test scores is the focus of professional learning. Expertise, according to Dall'Alba and Sandberg (2006), is a teacher's ability to learn from analysis of practice in collaboration with others using student results as the standard for excellence (pp. 388-389).

We propose a view of professional development that recognizes teachers as active professionals who engage in continuous improvement, reflect on their practices, and engage in knowledge construction and sharing through collaborative professional learning. This approach to professional learning places teachers at the center of learning. Such professional learning engages them in inquiry-based and problem-based conversations focused on the challenges they face in their own teaching and student learning. Using their collective expertise, teachers have the capacity to solve most of the challenges they face in ways that are contextually appropriate and frequently independent of additional resources.

RATIONALE

Complex, intractable problems exist in all communities. However, also within those communities are situations in which these problems do not exist. For example, among schools and districts with large populations of high-poverty students who have traditionally underperformed in school, there are classrooms and schools, with similar populations, where students succeed. For nearly two decades, researchers have asked what sets these successful classrooms or schools apart. The result of such an inquiry is often the identification of "best practices" that describe what works in a particular program, school, or district. These practices, according to Sparks, are disseminated and adopted by districts or schools that "prescribe them to teachers who are monitored carefully for compliance" (2007, p. 185).

Yet, little dramatic change is evident as a result of this approach to school improvement. Because schools are so different from one another in terms of staff and student characteristics, resources, parental and community support and involvement, and leadership, the assumption that a solution that worked in one school or classroom is going to work in another is faulty. That assumption has proven unsuccessful as a means for rapid and even lasting change in the nation's public schools. A more appropriate approach is to maintain the focus on what works within the defined community and to figure out how the community wants to use the information to improve its own results. Information of this sort is usu-

ally not transferable across communities. Tapping teacher expertise within a school increases the chance of identifying solutions that can be adopted throughout the school, sustained for longer periods of time, and implemented without extensive additional resources.

Schools, like all communities, have intractable, deeply embedded problems that impede student learning. If it were possible to find solutions to those problems within schools, schools would be less dependent, better able to implement solutions that fit their unique context, and develop the capacity to use the same solution-finding process repeatedly to solve other problems as they emerged.

The challenge then is to identify solutions that the community has already developed in order to solve or avoid certain problems. In their work with Save the Children to address childhood malnutrition in Vietnam in the 1990s, Jerry and Monique Sternin implemented a process called amplifying positive deviance to help communities quickly and effectively solve their complex problems. Positive deviants, according to Pascale and Sternin, discover "indigenous sources of change" (2005, p. 1). "We believe there are people in your company or group who are already doing things in a radically better way. The process we advocate seeks to bring the isolated success strategies of these 'positive deviants' into the mainstream" (p. 1). Positive deviants, according to Sternin, "are people whose behaviors and practices produce solutions to problems that others in the group who have access to exactly the same resources have not been able to solve. We want to identify these people because they provide demonstrable evidence that solutions to the problem already exist within the community" (Sparks, 2004, p. 46).

As teachers learn and work together in

collaborative teams, they share expertise, construct knowledge and refine practice, and shape their beliefs about teaching and learning. They explore, inquire, research, solve problems, and serve simultaneously as both teacher and learner. Evidence strongly suggests that when teachers collaborate within a school about instruction, curriculum, assessment, and students and set goals for collaborative professional learning, both teaching and student learning improve.

Many approaches to school improvement, according to Sparks, have little regard for the "intelligence and capacities that already reside within schools" (2007, pp. 185-186). External solutions have limited deep impact on teaching and learning within schools and only temporary impact on student learning. National reform efforts, district reform efforts, and even school reform efforts driven by external experts typically lack the consistency, constancy, and intensity of support to become more than temporary solutions to deeply rooted problems. Sadly, few leave behind a teaching staff with the capacity to create their own initiatives to solve subsequent problems related to practice. Few consider the most significant consequences of so many externally driven solutions — the loss of teacher morale and professional judgment, and collective responsibility and increased dependency on external forces to improve what teachers do in their classrooms each day.

Sternin, in an interview with Sparks (2004), presents a convincingly simple point about the impact of external solutions. "It is natural for people to resist when someone tells them what to do. That's part of human nature. It's like the human immune system's rejection of anything it senses as foreign. It's the same thing as the psychological and emotional levels when an external solution is imposed on us. When the solution comes from within the system, the immune response isn't activated," stresses Sternin. "People learn best when they discover things for themselves. Knowledge is usually insufficient to change behavior. It is our own discoveries that change behavior" (p. 48).

Empowered teams recognize that there are appropriate times for seeking outside expertise. When we respect the intellect of the individuals holding the problem, then we have confidence that they know when their solutions aren't working and that they need to seek outside expertise. Empowered teams also recognize the outside world as a constant source of enrichment and new knowledge. Empowered teams also know that improving practice will always require learning new knowledge, new skills, and new dispositions. Individuals can grow through on-the-job practical learning or through expert learning that they seek from outside the school to assist them with their efforts.

SUPPORTING EVIDENCE

In the last decade, evidence to support the value of shared expertise on improving student learning is mounting. The value is placed in two areas. Teachers' expertise increases and instruction improves when teaching becomes a shared responsibility and everyone views themselves as teachers and learners. When this condition characterizes the environment in which teachers work, student learning improves. Similar arguments have been made for principal collaboration and sharing of expertise.

Some forms of professional development block teachers from developing and exercising their professional expertise. Hargreaves distinguishes between two forms of professional development. "Separate communities, separate teachers, separate development — this is nothing less than an apartheid of professional development and school improvement, " he writes (2003, p. 191). He finds that in districts with poor student performance and with large concentrations of high-poverty and minority students, teacher professional development is characterized as focusing on ensuring teachers implement tightly scripted programs and on the monitoring of teacher implementation. In these situations, teacher professional judgment and teacher professionalism are removed in favor of strict fidelity to a scripted or tightly monitored program of instruction.

On the other hand, teachers in more affluent school districts serving large populations of high-performing students and with less diversity among students experience professional development that can be characterized as extending teachers' content knowledge, use of professional judgment, and developing local solutions to problems. Affluent schools enjoy flexibility, autonomy, freedom from monitoring, and the ability to network extensively. They are magnets of excellence, opportunity, organizational learning, and success. They are members of the knowledge society, creating it and contributing to its dissemination.

In an attempt to use professional development to address some of the knottiest problems facing schools, educators have inadvertently created a gap of a more significant kind. As a result of his study of schools, Hargreaves (2003) found a pattern in the professional development that is predominant in schools that experience significant change. Schools that use a professional learning community approach to professional development are renewed from within, not fixed from the outside. Frequently, the stimulus for change is exerted from outside the school. Yet the path to change and the energy for change in these schools emerges from within. This drive for change emerges when teachers themselves take up the standard of improvement and become its champions. Change happens when teachers' professional judgment is recognized and trusted by system leaders. Change happens when teachers have permission to explore options and take risks. Change happens when the school community joins hand in hand with teachers to create the school every educator wants for his or her children. Finally, change happens because the conversations and the work in schools shift from teaching to learning, from management to individual students, from budget to possibilities, from deficit to assets, from blame to action (Killion, 2006).

A school system's approach to professional learning influences how teachers structure learning for their students. If teachers of poor students and teachers of affluent students experience different kinds of professional learning, those teachers will likely structure different kinds of learning experiences for their students. Professional learning that develops teachers' capacity to inquire, share expertise, and solve complex problems is essential to creating systems of learning that engage students in inquiry, the sharing of learning, and the ability to solve complex problems. "I believe that the first step in reforming the learning experiences of young people is to reform the learning experiences for the adults responsible for young people's education" (Barth, 2001, p. 75).

Allowing solutions to emerge from within engenders commitment within the community rather than resistance. "When identification of a superior method is imposed, not self-discovered, cries of 'We're not them' or 'It just won't work here' predictably limit acceptance. By contrast, a design that allows a community to learn from its own hidden wisdom is, among other things, respectful. Innovators and adopters share the same DNA. Community members invest sweat equity in discovering the positive deviants, and, in the process, they become partners to change" (Pascale & Sternin, p. 3). Positive deviance, according to Pascale (2000), involves "scaling up a solution that is already working in the community. … The design was aimed to discover what was already working against all odds, rather than engineer a solution based on an external solution" (pp. 176-177).

Deborah Meier calls for reinventing the teacher professional so that "teachers actively, collaboratively, and systematically seek answers to their own dilemmas of practice and construct professional knowledge rooted, not only in educational theory, but also in lived classroom experiences" (Wood, 2007, p. 709).

Huberman (1993) suggested that centering teacher communities within teams of teachers who share students or curriculum might be the best way to tap teacher expertise. Orienting teacher learning in teams, departments, or grade levels "where people have concrete things to tell one another and concrete instructional help to provide one another" and "where the contexts of instruction actually overlap" (p. 45) may make the most sense.

This form of professional interaction, says Wood (2007), "requires a professional development agenda that doesn't simply equip teachers with techniques, but widens their professional responsibility and hones their professional judgment. It is an agenda, much like that of other self-regulating professions to foster commitment, autonomy, collegiality, and efficacy" (p. 709).

If this new approach to professionalism is unleashed without the cultural and normative barriers so prevalent in schools, and "if teachers accept the primary responsibility for growing in expertise and professional judgment so they can respond effectively to student needs," (p. 710) schools will become places in which no student or teacher can fail.

When teachers work together, they both learn and refine their practice. One approach to building and tapping teacher expertise is through collective inquiry about practice and student learning. In an early study about teacher learning communities in schools experiencing court-ordered desegregation, Little (1987) found that schools with professional norms of collegiality and experimentation were better able to respond to major innovations and improve student achievement." Teachers who have worked together closely over a period of years celebrate their accomplishments by pointing to gains in the achievement, behavior, and attitude of students. … Over time, teachers who work closely together on matters of curriculum and instruction find themselves better equipped for classroom work. They are frequently and credibly recognized for their professional capabilities and interests. And they take pride in professional relationships that withstand differences in viewpoint and occasional conflict" (pp. 493-494).

In McLaughlin's and Talbert's (2001) study of secondary schools, the researchers found a difference between weak and strong professional cultures. In strong professional cultures, teacher expertise was valued, shared, and tapped. Teachers explored their individual and collective views about subject-matter teaching and frequently challenged one another's practices and displayed a collective responsibility for student success. In weak professional cultures, teachers' work remained private and unchallenged. Teacher expertise also remained an untapped source of learning for members of weak professional cultures, and solutions that had been discovered in one teacher's classroom to complex problems related to student learning were kept private.

Schmoker (2006) confirms that traditional forms of training provide little support for teachers to translate their learning into practice. He recommends that the best form of teacher learning is one that promotes teachers' interdependence rather than dependence on an external expert, one that engages teachers in frequent analysis of data and use of data to plan instruction, one in which teachers work in teams, and one in which teachers share experience and practice. Gains, he claims, result from internal expertise, shared and refined as teachers collaborate about their practices. Schmoker urges leaders to "honor and empower teachers and their intelligence, capturing the vast reserves of expertise in any team and school" (p. 114).

In an extensive analysis of teacher professional development and teacher professional community, Little (2006) concludes that "schools that exhibit a high level of success with students, sometimes against considerable odds, tend to support consistent portraits of work environments conducive to teacher learning. In these schools, teacher learning arises out of close involvement with students and their work; shared responsibility for student progress; access to new knowledge about learning and teaching; sensibly organized time; **access to the expertise of colleagues inside and outside the school** (author's emphasis); focused and timely feedback on individual performance and on aspects of classroom or school practice; and an overall ethos in

which teacher learning is valued and professional community is cultivated" (p. 22). Teacher collaboration, shared responsibility, shared expertise, and continuous learning rise again as features of schools where students succeed.

IN PRACTICE

Teachers learn from multiple sources. They learn from expertise within their schools and school systems and from expertise they find outside their schools and school systems. Teachers report, however, that they learn the most from one another. However, too frequently schools have sought solutions to problems from outside the school before tapping the expertise that already exists within. In every school, even those viewed as troubled, there are teachers doing outstanding work. The real challenge to getting significant improvement in these schools is tapping the expertise of those teachers and creating a culture that fosters the value of learning with and from each other. At times, teachers recognize that their learning needs to be bolstered by experts who are not a part of their daily community of practice. They recognize that their own communities must be enriched frequently by new findings and new perspectives that come from beyond their schools. Teachers' expertise is honed when teachers acknowledge the desire to have an external perspective to stretch their own knowledge and perspective.

Schmoker (2006) offers one example of this process of tapping expertise from within. "One high school English department began to pick each other's brains on how to most effectively teach a clear, specific standard, something magical happened — even in focused four-minute meetings," he writes. "They began to share and refine the collective wealth of what they already knew.

They found that they could create lessons that allowed record numbers of students to master the most sophisticated writing skills, one lesson at a time in their high-poverty, high-minority school" (p. 115).

Another possible approach to tapping internal expertise comes from applying the amplifying positive deviance approach to school challenges. As previously described in this chapter, amplifying positive deviance depends on the expertise within the community to address problems that are deeply rooted within the community. Amplifying positive deviance is built on the premise that within every community some members of the community are in fact applying strategies that either solve or prevent the problem by using resources already available to all members of the community. By discovering those strategies, sharing the practices across all members and monitoring results, the community can eliminate problems. The challenge of amplifying positive deviance lies in identifying the problem with enough specificity that the results can be seen and the successful strategies can be identified.

In a very limited examination of schools and districts that applied some of the tenets of the positive deviance inquiry approach, NSDC identified schools and districts that sought expertise within. Without ever recognizing they were applying the concepts of positive deviance, each of the four schools and two districts identified successful practices and shared those practices throughout the system (Richardson, 2004).

One particularly powerful exemplar of tapping expertise within a community is the story of Mary Dunbar Barksdale, a 3rd-grade teacher in the Brazosport Independent School District in Texas. The district assistant superintendent, Pat Davenport, discovered that Barksdale's

3rd-grade students at Velasco Elementary School were achieving unexpected results despite the fact that 94% lived in poverty. As Davenport investigated, she discovered that Barksdale "closely examined the results of her students' tests, identified their problem areas, retaught, and retested until they achieved the desired level" (Richardson, p. 64). "Davenport realized Barksdale's process could be replicated easily by other teachers. The most logical group to learn the process would be teachers at Velasco, so Barksdale began there. Over the next several years, all of Velasco's teachers began to experience the same high results with their children" (p. 64). Soon Barksdale's practice was spread across the school and district, and the achievement gap was closed. Without any special external program or special resources, the expertise of one teacher was amplified across classrooms and schools to solve the perplexing achievement gap problem.

Citing an example of teachers solving a complex problem within their school by tapping into their own expertise, Schmoker (2006) says:

"Teachers from Havasupai Elementary School (Lake Havasu City, Ariz.) were returning from yet another much-hyped but time-wasting workshop. In the van driving home, they began to construct, on a yellow pad, a new reading program. It was largely based on **what they already knew** (author's emphasis) but hadn't had a chance to organize or refine — the need to greatly increase time spent on meaningful reading and writing activities. Grade-level teams, with support from the principal, began to collaborate regularly and to conduct frequent common assessments, which helped them to see the impact of their efforts, by grade level, and to make adjustments to instruction. That year there were significant, and in some grades dramatic, gains in reading.

The principal, seeing the results, wondered aloud why they haven't always done business this way" (p. 105).

Solutions to complex, intractable problems exist in every school community. These solutions emerge when teachers share and construct expertise in regular collaboration about teaching and learning. If every school could solve persistent problems of student learning such as the achievement gap, students would learn, schools would be more successful, and teacher expertise would be recognized and more regularly tapped, which would increase teacher morale, inventiveness, and professional judgment.

CONCLUSION

No complex social problem can be solved from the outside. We see evidence of this in our world today. The attempt to use practices that are successful in very different contexts to solve a problem in any environment or culture yields short-term gains that are eroded through disenfranchisement, disempowering, and dishonesty.

When we "deliver" staff development to fix a problem, fill a knowledge void, and alter behaviors, we are ignoring and mistreating teachers, our most powerful resources. Instead, we want to move to a system that engages in respectful dialogue and problem-solving processes, constructing knowledge rather than attempting to transmit or transfer it. "If every student is to have a competent teacher, then virtually all their teachers must be learning virtually all the time," asserts Sparks (1998). "While that learning will occasionally happen in workshops and courses, most of it will occur as teachers plan lessons together, examine their students' work to find ways to improve it, observe one another teach, and plan improvements based on various data. Those of us concerned about teacher expertise must take leadership in designing such a system for learning" (p. 2).

If school and district leaders and teachers themselves can shift their beliefs and normative practices so that accountability for the highest quality of teaching rests with teachers and is deeply embedded in the culture of schools, "teachers, as they confront difficult problems with student learning, might be less tempted to turn away from these problems, to give up on them, to find others to blame for them, or to wait for others to produce solutions. Instead, they might be more likely to turn to one another, take collective responsibility, and actively pursue effective solutions," suggests Wood (2007). "No recipe for change could promise more than the revitalization and empowerment of those whose work directly affects what children actually experience in their classrooms — their teachers" (p. 737).

"When teachers recognize that knowledge for improvement is something they can generate, rather than something that must be handed to them by so-called experts, they are on a new professional trajectory," state Hiebert and Stigler (2004). "They are on the way to build a true profession of teaching, a profession in which members take responsibility for steady and lasting improvement" (p. 15). In schools where "teacher expertise is tapped, we are building a new professional culture, one that moves from a 'culture of dependency' that disempowers teachers and is a barrier to smart, constructive effort" (Fullan & Hargreaves, p. 24) to one that enhances their professional responsibility and judgment.

REFERENCES

Barth, R. (2001). *Learning by heart.* San Francisco: Jossey-Bass.

Dall'Alba, G. & Sandberg, J. (2006). Unveiling professional development: A critical review of stage models. *Review of Educational Research, 76*(3), 383-412.

Elmore, R. & Burney, D. (1997). *Investing in teacher learning: Staff development and instructional improvement in Community School District #2, New York City.* Washington, DC: National Commission on Teaching and America's Future and Consortium for Policy Reform in Education.

Fullan, M. (2001). *The new meaning of educational change (3rd ed.).* New York: Teachers College Press.

Fullan, M. & Hargreaves, A. (1996). *What's worth fighting for in your school?* New York: Teachers College Press.

Hargreaves, A. (2003). *Teaching in the knowledge society.* New York: Teachers College Press.

Hiebert, J. & Stigler, J. (2004). A world of difference: Classrooms abroad provide lessons teaching math and science. *JSD, 25*(4), 10-15.

Huberman, M. (1993). The model of the independent artisan in teachers' professional relations. In J. Little & M. McLaughlin (Eds.), *Teachers' work: Individuals, colleagues, and contexts* (pp. 11-50). New York: Teachers College Press.

Killion, J. (2006, February). *Staff development to close the achievement gap.* Speech given to Kansas Staff Development Council.

Little, J.W. (1987). Teachers as colleagues: A research perspective. In V. Richardson-Koehler (Ed.), *The educators handbook* (pp. 491-518). London: Longman Group.

Little, J.W. (2006). *Professional community and professional development in the learning-centered school.* Best Practices

Working Paper. Washington, DC: National Education Association.

McLaughlin, M. & Talbert, J. (2001). *Professional communities and the work of high school teaching.* Chicago: University of Chicago Press.

Pascale, R. & Sternin, J. (2005). Your company's secret change agents. *Harvard Business Review,* Reprint R0505D.

Pascale, R. (2000). Herding butterflies. In R. Pascale, M. Milleman, & L., *Surfing on the edge of chaos* (pp. 175-181, 222-223, 284). New York: Crown.

Richardson, J. (2004). *From the inside out: Learning from the positive deviance in your organization* (pp. 125-145). Oxford, OH: NSDC.

Schmoker, M. (2006). *Results now: How we can achieve unprecedented improvement in teaching and learning.* Alexandria, VA: ASCD.

Sparks, D. (1998, April) Teacher expertise linked to student achievement. *Results,* 1.

Sparks, D. (2004). From hunger aid to school reform. An interview with Jerry Sternin. *JSD, 25*(1) 46-51.

Sparks, D. (2007). *Leading for results: Transforming teaching, learning, and relationships in schools* (2nd ed.). Thousand Oaks, CA: Corwin Press and NSDC.

Wood, D. (2007). Teachers' learning communities: Catalyst for change or a new infrastructure for the status quo? *Teachers College Record, 109*(3), 699-739.

York-Barr, J. & Duke, K. (2004). What do we know about teacher leadership? Findings from two decades of scholarship. *Review of Educational Research, 74*(3), 255-317.

"Individually, we are one drop. Together, we are an ocean."
— *Ryunosuke Satoro*

PRINCIPLE 8

COLLABORATION

Collaboration among educators builds shared
responsibility and improves student learning.

"**M**argaret plays well with others." Every parent takes great pride in receiving such notes from his or her child's kindergarten teacher. Margaret's parents post the message on the refrigerator as a constant reminder of Margaret's success. They know Margaret has already begun to demonstrate the skills to be successful beyond school one day.

However, as Margaret progresses through her education, she experiences fewer and fewer opportunities to practice teamwork and collaboration with other students. She sees little evidence that it is valued except perhaps in her physical education courses, and little evidence that it occurs among her teachers. Schools send subtle messages that "playing well with others" may not be as important as her kindergarten teacher and her parents once believed.

Yet, our experiences outside of school convey a different message. The Renaissance man has become the Renaissance team. *Marcus Welby* is now a team of doctors on *ER*, and *Magnum PI* is now a team of investigators on *CSI Miami*. If teamwork is necessary for success outside the classroom, then schools should prepare students to be part of such teams.

We are better together than we are individually. We have previously stated that students benefit when educators pool their expertise and that collaboration is a hallmark of high-quality professional learning.

"To advocate human conversation as the means to restore hope to the future is as simple as I can get," states Wheatley (2002). "But I've seen that there is no more powerful way to initiate significant change than to convene a conversation. When a community of people discovers that they share a concern, change begins. There is no power equal to a community discovering what it cares about" (p. 22).

There is no doubt that everyone wants all students to experience great teaching every day. We believe that this outcome is best achieved in schools where collaboration among educators is a priority. Educators need opportunities to share their strengths with and seek guidance from colleagues as they address challenges and solve problems. When teachers collaborate to jointly plan lessons and assessments, students in the same grade or course benefit from the collective expertise of all those teachers. And collaboration on lesson plans and assessments has a secondary benefit: Teaching is improved through the teachers' collective expertise that went into that lesson design. Schools will be far more likely to be able to provide great teaching for every student when collaboration among educators is routine and daily. In addition, when all educators in a school assume a collective responsibility for their own and students' success, we fulfill our moral commitment to children.

RATIONALE

Educators collaborate for a variety of reasons, including planning celebrations for staff members or students, planning events for the school, or scheduling events for the school community. However, we advocate for an additional purpose for educator collaboration — collaboration to plan and improve the learning that occurs in classrooms on a daily basis. When educators agree to collaborate to strengthen and support teaching and learning, all students benefit.

Collaboration among educators improves learning opportunities for students. In many schools, a culture of collaboration and collective responsibility is replacing the culture of isolation. Educators are recognizing that all students benefit when they pool

their expertise. They also realize that educating all students requires more knowledge and effort than any one individual educator possesses.

As school culture changes, so does professional learning. "The theory of individual professional growth has given way to a culture-centered approach toward professional learning aimed at collegial teams — learning and practicing together," suggest Wagner and Masden-Copas (2002). "Acknowledging that, 'unless teams of teachers improve together, schools never will' stresses the cultural approach toward improvement and change. The goal of professional development is the enculturation of a continuous improvement philosophy among teams of professionals rather than individual teachers. This can only occur in a healthy school culture designed to promote higher levels of professional collaboration, collegiality, and self-determination" (p. 43).

Teachers recognize the many benefits of collaboration. They feel less isolated, less alone, and more satisfied in their work. They are able to share expertise rather than withhold it. They acknowledge that there is an abundance rather than a scarcity of resources within their school. They report feeling a part of something that is larger than just their own classroom and can contribute to the well-being of the entire school. They feel more appreciated and valued by their colleagues and other school staff.

Teachers also know that the most important outcome of their collaboration is the collective responsibility shared among the school community to achieve their common purpose, student learning. The purpose of teacher collaboration is to ensure that all students, not just those within a few classrooms, succeed. Teachers who work in a community no longer struggle in private with the challenge of students meeting standards. Teachers view all students within a school as their responsibility.

"True learning communities are characterized by disciplined, professional collaboration and ongoing assessment. This is the surest most promising route to better school performance, and the reasons are compelling," says Schmoker (2005), citing Little. He continues, "Teachers do not learn best from outside experts or by attending conferences or implementing 'programs' installed by outsiders. Teachers learn best from other teachers, in settings where they literally teach each other the art of teaching. For this to happen, collaboration had to occur in a radically different way than most of what Little saw. Productive collaboration could not be casual or general; it was instead characterized by: 'Frequent, continuous, and increasingly concrete and precise talk about teaching practice … adequate to the complexities of teaching and capable of distinguishing one practice and its virtue from another' " (pp. 141-142).

District and school leaders have a responsibility to examine the research and evidence from practice that supports the benefits of collaboration. District and school leaders can study how other schools and school systems created time during the workday for teachers to collaborate that helped them learn the basics of collaborative work. Teachers can visit leading schools to study the structures, processes, and benefits of collaboration. Teachers can then go back to their own schools and experiment with various collaborative structures, and principals can provide formal support and facilitation to help teachers achieve productive collaboration. Ultimately, district and school leaders will see the benefits of student-centered collaboration and revamp school schedules and structures to ensure

that all teachers are members of collaborative professional learning teams focused on ensuring success of all students.

SUPPORTING EVIDENCE

As schools strive to improve student achievement, more and more are using professional development as their primary intervention. Beliefs and practices about good professional development are shifting. Research is pointing to the relationship between teachers who work together collaboratively and a resulting improvement in student learning. "Researchers point to an 'emerging consensus' regarding the kind of professional development most likely to improve teacher practice and thus student performance," suggest Miles, Odden, Fermanich, and Archibald (2005). "This consensus suggests that the highest impact professional development directly relates to the instructional content and material teachers use; takes place in their own schools and classrooms with coaching and ongoing feedback; and seeks to involve all teachers so that the learning for adults emphasizes schoolwide rather than individual capacity" (p. 9).

Research, best practice, and nationally recognized educators contribute supporting evidence for the collaboration principle. This case focuses on some of the benefits of collaboration including developing consistency in teaching, ownership for results, promoting continuous improvement of members, finding solutions to complex problems, assisting the newer members of the community, and increasing student learning.

Newmann and Wehlage (1995) identified commonalities among schools with disproportionately higher student performance in math, science, and social studies. These schools had staff members who formed learning communities, focused their attention on student work and assessment, and changed their instructional practices to improve their results with students. Common goals, consistent messages about learning objectives and methods, and collective responsibility, say Newmann and Wehlage, increase teacher efficacy. In addition, they believe that teachers' collaborative activity increases their technical competence and collective responsibility.

"Collaborative activity can enhance teachers' technical competence. As teachers work with students from increasingly diverse social backgrounds, and as the curriculum begins to demand more intellectual rigor, teachers require information, technical expertise, and social-emotional support far beyond the resources they can muster as individuals working alone. When teachers collaborate productively, they participate in reflective dialogue to learn more about professional issues; they observe and react to one another's teaching, curriculum, and assessment practices; and they engage in joint planning and curriculum development. By enriching teachers' technical and social resources, collaboration can make teaching more effective (Newmann & Wehlage, 1995, p. 31).

"… [C]learly shared purpose and collaboration contribute to collective responsibility: one's colleagues share responsibility for the quality of all students' achievement. This norm helps to sustain each teacher's commitment. A culture of collective responsibility puts more peer pressure and accountability on staff who may not have carried their fair share, but it can also ease the burden on teachers who have worked hard in isolation but who felt unable to help some students. In short, professional community within the teaching staff sharpens the educational focus and enhances the tech-

nical and social support that teachers need to be successful" (Newmann & Wehlage, 1995, p. 31).

Hord (2004) takes a definitive stand on the power of collaboration when integrated into the learning community process. Hord concludes that both staff and students benefit from the effects of professional learning communities in schools: Teachers are less isolated, share in the collective responsibility for student success, and have higher morale and less absenteeism, students in these schools also have less absenteeism, greater academic gains, and smaller achievement gaps between students of different backgrounds.

In their extensive study about features of effective professional development, Garet, Porter, Desimone, Birman, and Yoon (2001) report that, "Research on teacher learning shows that fruitful opportunities to learn new teaching methods share several core features: (a) *ongoing (measured in years) collaboration of teachers for purposes of planning with* (authors' emphasis) (b) the explicit goal of improving students' achievement of clear learning goals, (c) anchored by attention to students' thinking, the curriculum, and pedagogy, with (d) access to alternative ideas and methods and opportunities to observe these in action and to reflect on the reasons for their effectiveness" (p. 917).

Little (1990) contributes early and definitive research about the value of teacher collaboration. In her study of teacher work, she found much of what teachers did when they meet thinly disguised as genuine collaboration. She concludes that regular, authentic "joint work" focused on clear and explicit goals for student learning "pays off richly in the form of higher quality solutions to instructional problems, increased teacher confidence, and, not surprisingly, remarkable gains in student achievement"

(Schmoker, 2006, p. 178).

In a study of 32 elementary schools that compares strategies of schools that closed the achievement gap in California, Symonds (2003) concludes that those schools that most distinguished themselves engaged in a far more intense set of professional development strategies than schools that were merely making progress. In the best gap-closing schools, teachers engaged in frequent dialogue about student learning and instruction. They discussed student performance evidence several times a month or weekly. Teachers in the best gap-closing schools worked more closely with school leaders, engaged in inquiry about the nature of the achievement gap to plan appropriate professional development, discussed evidence generated from both externally and internally developed assessments of student learning, and used data from assessments to refine instruction. In describing this study, Little (2006) summarizes the strategy: "In effect, these schools developed a collective capacity for *formative assessment* of student progress as a resource for their own decision making, although they credit the need periodically to take stock of whether and how well students have mastered particular concepts and skills (*summative assessment*)" (p. 11).

"School systems … would be well advised to name knowledge sharing as a core value — to label it explicitly, which they do not now do — and to begin to work on the barriers and procedures to dramatically increase its use," posits Fullan (2001, p. 105). Sparks (1998) summarizes both the importance of professional development and the particular form of it that will improve student learning:

"If every student is to have a competent teacher, then virtually all of their teachers must be learning virtually all the time. While that learning will occasionally happen in workshops and courses, most of it will occur as teachers plan lessons together, examine their students' work to find ways to improve it, observe one another teach, and plan improvements based on various data. Those of us concerned about teacher expertise must take leadership in designing such a system for learning" (p. 2).

The benefits of collaboration reach beyond the experienced teacher with extensive experience and expertise to share. McRobbie (2000) identifies one of the most powerful reasons for supporting collaborative planning among educators: "Regular time for teacher collaboration can help ensure that lessons are more highly polished, students' needs are better met, and curriculum is cohesive from year to year" (p. 6). Lewis and Paik (2001) argue that new teachers are better served in schools organized as professional communities where members collaborate to promote educator and student success. They write, "The research indicates that quality schools generally have a stable, professional community of experienced teachers who share norms, values, goals, and a common focus on student learning. The school culture fosters among staff a willingness to collaborate and an openness to reflection and new ideas directed toward supporting high student achievement" (p. 6).

In the end, what the National Education Association Foundation for the Improvement of Education (2000) reports in its study of teacher collaboration in schools offers the most compelling reason for embracing collaboration as a key tenet of effective professional learning. "Schools where teachers focus on student work, interact with colleagues to plan how to improve their teaching, and continuously bring new skills and knowledge to bear on their practice are also schools that produce the best results for children" (p. 1).

IN PRACTICE

Schmoker (2004) writes, "Thousands of schools and even entire districts can attest to the power of these structures for promoting first incremental and then cumulatively dramatic and enduring improvements in teaching and learning. A short list would include Central Park East, in New York's Harlem; Bennet-Kew Elementary School in Inglewood, California; Warm Springs Elementary School on the Warm Springs Reservation in Oregon; Crossroads Elementary School in Norfolk, Virginia; Mather Elementary School in Boston; Kerman Unified Schools in rural, high-poverty California; Oak Park Schools near Detroit; Boones Mill School in rural Virginia; and many more. These schools and districts have made substantive, enduring gains in achievement, largely on the strength of well-structured, goal-oriented learning teams and communities"(p. 431).

Collaboration is a powerful notion, yet the realities of practice continue to challenge schools. Guskey writes about the unfulfilled promise of the kind of professional development in which "teachers work together, reflect on their practice, exchange ideas, and share strategies" (Schmoker, 2004, p. 430). But numerous issues stand in the way of achieving that kind of professional development: time and schedules, teacher will and belief in the potential of collaboration, and teachers' understanding about how to structure productive collaborative time.

"… [F]aculties must stop making excuses for failing to collaborate," contend DuFour, Eaker, and DuFour (2005). "Few educators publicly assert that working in isolation is the best strategy for improving schools. Instead, they give reasons why it is impossible for them to work together: 'We just can't find the time.' 'Not everyone on the staff has endorsed the idea.' 'We need more training in collaboration.' But the number of schools that have created truly collaborative cultures proves that such barriers are not insurmountable" (p. 39).

Gideon (2002) identifies what is essential to ensure that collaborative learning produces the desired outcomes for students. He writes: "Two factors are necessary to successfully implement a more collegial model of school organization. The collaboration, at least at first, must address issues that teachers find immediately useful and be structured into the regular teacher workday. Many collaborations have failed because the innovations or recommendations, although ultimately benefiting teachers and students, were not immediately evident or because teachers were often asked to meet before or after their regular workday — when they were tired and had other responsibilities to fulfill. If we truly believe that teacher collaboration is key to school improvement, it must be part of the regular work of teachers and administrators, teacher recommendations must actually be implemented, and teachers must be publicly recognized for their success" (p. 42).

Schools and districts can attest to the power of these structures for promoting first incremental and then cumulatively dramatic and enduring improvements in teaching and learning. These schools and districts have made substantive, enduring gains in achievement, largely on the strength of well-structured, goal-oriented learning teams and communities.

A variety of natural structures within schools support ongoing collaboration about teaching and learning. Grade-level, department, course-specific, subject-based, or whole school teams meet regularly in most schools to provide ongoing collaboration. For example, Trimble (2003) suggests,

"Departmental teams provide the support that teachers need to learn new skills and varied perspectives from team members who teach the same subject to a wide range of students. Specifically, teachers work collaboratively in departmental teams to analyze student data, determine content, write assessment questions, and design teaching strategies and time lines" (p. 35).

Working conditions for educators should follow the pattern of practices in other professions. Troen and Boles (2003) write: "Yet, in an era when automobiles are built by teams, and doctors and lawyers practice their profession in cultures of collaboration, teachers are still isolated sole practitioners, receiving little supervision, ineffective mentoring, and no meaningful professional development" (p. 1). In the fields of medicine and law, doctors and lawyers used to work alone as sole practitioners, consulting one another only when a challenging case emerged. Many of today's doctors and lawyers work in teams. Doctors collaborate with specialists about patient needs. Interns and residents participate in rounds where they share patient information with their colleagues. Lawyers meet to dissect cases and determine strategies. Yet many teachers still cling to a view of teaching as a private, isolated act. Perhaps in another 10 years, teacher isolation will no longer be possible because of the ever-changing nature of our schools and the demands placed on educators.

Working collaboratively can be challenging, and it can also be the most rewarding form of work. Schools that are serious about collaboration will face two hurdles. The first hurdle is time. Many school staff members argue that it is impossible to create teacher schedules that enable collaborative planning and learning, yet an increasing number of schools have schedules that permit regular and frequent collaboration. For most, finding the time is more a matter of commitment than of deliberation. We hope that, within the next 10 years, schools will have access to software programs that will allow them to create schedules that serve students and educators equally well.

The second hurdle relates to process. There are those who believe that collaboration merely means putting teachers in groups. Collaborative professional learning is not simply a matter of finding the time and creating teams of teachers. If the focus of teachers' collaborative work is not on improving teaching and learning, results will be meager. Teams benefit from having protocols, processes, and practice in collaborative learning designs such as lesson study, critical friends groups, data analysis, assessment writing, and other critical areas. Joyce (2004) states it simply, "… many folks lack the tools to engage in either small-group collaboration or whole school action research" (p. 79). When teachers know how to use their time productively, set goals, and choose designs that are aligned with their goals, they are more likely to accomplish those goals.

Districts and schools can support increased collaboration and its results by investing in the development of teachers' collaborative skills and in teacher leaders who will facilitate collaboration and learning in order to improve teaching and learning. With a clear understanding of this specific challenge, Sparks (2002) writes, "Schools make a major mistake when they settle for creating team structures. The real challenge is developing teams with high 'group IQ,' teams that are effective in working together to solve problems and to renew their school. We cannot settle for merely creating team structures. We must work to address the challenge of developing high-performance teams that are focused on essential questions of teaching and learning" (p. 25).

So Hargreaves (2003) distinguishes among several different levels of collaboration among educators — congeniality, contrived congeniality, and collegiality. Congeniality describes a faculty where staff members are cordial with one another but conversation topics are mostly unrelated to what happens in classrooms. Collegiality describes the interactions among faculty members that center on their work. McLaughlin and Talbert (2001) discovered this distinction in their work, too.

To promote change through collaboration, Wheatley (2002) offers some simple yet powerful ideas any group of educators can use to increase the effectiveness of their time together. "There is no power greater than a community discovering what it cares about," she posits. She continues with these recommendations:

- Ask "What's possible?" not "What's wrong?" Keep asking.
- Notice what you care about.
- Assume that many others share your dreams.
- Be brave enough to start a conversation that matters. Talk to people you know. Talk to people you don't know. Talk to people you never talk to.
- Be intrigued by the differences you hear. Expect to be surprised. Treasure curiosity more than certainty.
- Invite everybody who cares to work on what's possible to participate. Acknowledge that everyone is an expert about something. Know that creative solutions come from new connections.
- Remember, you don't fear people whose story you know. Real listening always brings people closer together. Trust that meaningful conversations can change your world. Rely on human goodness. Stay together (p. 145).

CONCLUSION

The notion of teachers working in collaboration is not new to education. In 1975, Lortie in the seminal work, *Schoolteacher*, recognizes that teachers are more satisfied in their work when they share ideas and experiences. In 1990, Little's research on teacher work highlights the importance of collaboration. When teachers plan, design, research, evaluate, and prepare teaching materials together, students learn. Such simple effort — teachers teaching one another the practice of teaching — leads to what has to be one of the most salient lists of benefits in educational literature:

- Higher-quality solutions to instructional problems;
- Increased confidence among faculty;
- Increased ability to support one another's strengths and to accommodate weaknesses;
- More systematic assistance to beginning teachers; and
- The ability to examine an expanded pool of ideas, methods, and materials.

In combination, these elements can't help but produce gains in student achievement. The value to both teachers and students of increased collaboration and collective responsibility is noteworthy, yet not fully implemented. Perhaps Schmoker (2003) says it best when he acknowledges that, "It is time to close the gap between what we know and what we do to promote learning. It is still the rare school that recognizes that teachers, working together, have the capacity — right now — to improve instruction. We need to give them this opportunity," he recommends. "And then, just as regularly, we need to honor and celebrate each team's success as its members develop and share better lessons and strategies with their colleagues. It is no overstatement to say that in most schools, such practices would yield immense, often immediate benefits" (p. 39).

Sparks reinforces the urgency about increased collaboration among educators. "[I]f all students — black, white, rich, and poor — are to acquire deep understanding; develop the ability to work in teams and independently; and seek, through their concern about others, to contribute meaningfully to the public good, teachers must pursue deep and continuous professional learning," asserts Sparks (2004). "To achieve these outcomes, we will need to develop teachers who regularly exercise professional judgment, who can work in networks and teams, who can establish sustaining relationships with students and other teachers, who draw on research, and who make decisions based on shared data" (p. 305).

REFERENCES

DuFour, R. & Burnette, B. (2002). Pull out negativity by its roots. *Journal of Staff Development, 23*(3), 27-30.

DuFour, R., Eaker, R., & DuFour, R. (Eds.). (2005). *On common ground: The power of professional learning communities.* Bloomington, IN: Solution Tree.

Fullan, M. (2001). *Leading in a culture of change.* San Francisco: Jossey-Bass.

Fullan, M. & Hargreaves, A. (1996). *What's worth fighting for in your school?* New York: Teachers College Press.

Garet, M.S., Porter, A.C., Desimone, L., Birman, B.B., & Yoon, K.S. (2001). What makes professional development effective? Results from a national sample of teachers. *American Educational Research Journal, 38*(4), 915-945.

Gideon, B.H. (2002). Supporting a collaborative culture. *Principal Leadership, 3*(1), 41-44.

Hargreaves, A. (2003). *Teaching in the knowledge society: Education in the age of insecurity.* New York: Teachers College Press.

Hord, S.M. (Ed.). (2004). *Learning together, leading together: Changing schools through professional learning communities.* New York: Teachers College Press and NSDC.

Joyce, B. (2004). How are professional learning communities created? *Phi Delta Kappan, 86*(1), 76-83.

Lewis, A. & Paik, S. (2001). *Add it up: Using research to improve education for low-income and minority students.* Washington, DC: Poverty & Race Research Action Council.

Little, J.W. (1990). The persistence of privacy: Autonomy and initiative in teachers' professional relations. *Teachers College Record, 91*(4), 509-36.

Little, J.W. (2006). *Professional community and professional development in the learning-centered school.* Best Practices Working Paper. Washington, DC: National Education Association.

Lortie, D. (1975). *Schoolteacher: A sociological study.* Chicago: University of Chicago Press.

McLaughlin, M. & Talbert, J. (2001). *Professional communities and the work of high school teaching.* Chicago: University of Chicago Press.

McRobbie, J. (2000). *Career-long teacher development: Policies that make sense.* San Francisco: WestEd.

Miles, K.H., Odden, A., Fermanich, M., & Archibald, S. (2005). *Inside the black box: School district spending on professional development in education.* Washington, DC: The Finance Project.

NEA Foundation for the Improvement of Education. (2000). *Engaging public support for teachers' professional development.* Washington, DC: Author. Downloaded March 28, 2007. www.neafoundation.org/publications/engaging.htm#case

Newmann, F.M. & Wehlage, G.G. (1995). *Successful school restructuring.* Madison, WI: Center on Organization and Restructuring of Schools, School of Education, University of Wisconsin-Madison.

Schmoker, M. (2002). Up and away. *Journal of Staff Development, 24*(2), 10-13.

Schmoker, M. (2003, February 12). Planning for failure? *Education Week, 22*(22), 39.

Schmoker, M. (2004). Tipping point: From feckless reform to substantive instructional improvement. *Phi Delta Kappan, 85*(6), 424-432.

Schmoker, M. (2005). No turning back. In R. DuFour, R. Eaker, & R. DuFour (Eds.), *On common ground* (pp. 135-153). Bloomington, IN: Solution Tree.

Schmoker, M. (2006). *Results now: How we can achieve unprecedented improvements in teaching and learning.* Alexandria, VA: ASCD.

Sparks, D. (1998, April). Teacher expertise linked to student learning. *Results,* 2.

Sparks, D. (2002). Dreaming all that we might realize. *ENC Focus, 9*(1), 24-25.

Sparks, D. (2004, December). The looming danger of a two-tiered professional development system. *Phi Delta Kappan, 86*(4), 304-306.

Symonds, K. (2003). *After the test: How schools are using data to close the achievement gap.* San Francisco: Bay Area School Reform Collaborative.

Trimble, S. (2003). Between reform and improvement: In the classroom. *Principal Leadership, 1*(1), 35-39.

Troen, V. & Boles, K.C. (2003). We're still leaving the teachers behind. *The Teachers.net Gazette,* http://teachers.net/gazette/APR03/troenboles.html

Wagner, C. & Masden-Copas, P. (2002). An audit of the culture starts with two handy tools. *Journal of Staff Development, 23*(3), 42-43.

Wheatley, M. (2002). *Turning to one another: Simple conversations to restore hope to the future.* San Francisco: Berrett-Koehler.

OUR VISION

As we consider the eight principles outlined in the previous chapters, we imagine how they will influence the field of professional learning in the next decade. As these principles guide professional learning decisions in schools and school systems over the next 10 years, we will begin to see concrete shifts in professional learning practices. This chapter describes those shifts and what the changes will look like. These shifts and evidence that they are occurring can serve as benchmarks that schools and school systems are moving closer to professional learning that makes a difference in leading, teaching, and learning.

From inservice education and staff/professional development to professional learning.

Inservice as well as staff and professional development served a purpose in the evolution of our profession. But today, we advocate for a transition to professional learning. *Professional* as contrasted with *staff* signifies that everyone who works in education on behalf of students is a professional and that it is the responsibility of a professional to continue to advance knowledge, skills, and dispositions. *Learning* as contrasted with *development* or *growth* signifies that all educators have responsibilities to identify areas where students are not successful, and identify the knowledge and strategies that they need to address those deficiencies. In other words, professionals continue to learn in order to perform their jobs at the highest levels. Professional learning will achieve its potential only when the profession embraces the principles of leadership, teacher expertise, and collaboration.

From individual learning to team-based, schoolwide learning.

While there are benefits to individualized professional learning, team-based and schoolwide learning offer greater benefits. The interest of ensuring the success of all students is better served by team-based and schoolwide learning. If one teacher learns something that is helpful to him or her, then that teacher's students benefit. But when a team or an entire faculty learns together, an entire grade level or an entire school benefits. When the profession embraces the principles of diversity, focus, impact, and teacher expertise, team-based and schoolwide professional learning will increase the impact on student learning.

From focusing on increasing the number of staff development days or periods to restructuring the workday of all educators to ensure daily learning experiences.

If states, districts, and schools continue to talk about finding more time in terms of days and hours for professional development, they will not realize the impact of the most effective model of professional learning. In the next decade, we want conversations to begin with the question of how to restructure the school year and day so that learning with colleagues is a mandatory part of every workday for every educator. From there, the conversation can focus on the most effective use of the time and the role of external assistance and knowledge in supporting the highest performance and learning for all educators and their students. When the profession embraces the principles of leadership, planning, and collaboration, the reconstituted workday will produce results previously deemed impossible.

From focusing on credit-based relicensure/recertification systems to performance-based systems.

Counting hours for recertification

emphasizes a process rather than an outcome. We want to shift away from ensuring there are highly-qualified teachers in every classroom to ensuring there is high-quality teaching in every classroom. We do this by creating systems that award licenses to and renew licenses of educators who demonstrate the knowledge, skills, and dispositions necessary to provide skillful leadership and quality teaching in all schools for all students. When the profession embraces the principles of leadership, planning, impact, and teacher expertise, every student will experience high-quality instruction every day.

From individual teacher, school, or district professional development plans to effective professional learning embedded into team, school, and district improvement plans.

Professional development permeates every systematic improvement effort of every team, school, and district office. New initiatives will not be successfully implemented nor will goals be attained without investing in the knowledge, skills, and dispositions of the responsible individuals. Professional learning becomes the strategy for achieving the goals set for students by teams, school faculty, and district leaders. Professional learning is only as powerful as the district and school goals it is designed to achieve. When the profession embraces the principles of diversity, planning, focus, impact, and collaboration, powerful plans will produce results never before experienced.

From a view of professional development as an expenditure to professional learning as an investment.

The response to professional learning is different when all stakeholders view it as a critical investment in the future of

FROM ...	TO ...
Inservice education and staff/professional development	Professional learning
Individual learning	Team-based and schoolwide learning
Increasing the number of staff development days or periods	Restructuring the workday of all educators to ensure daily learning experiences
Credit-based relicensure/recertification systems	Performance-based systems
Separate individual teacher, school, or district professional development plans	Effective professional learning embedded into team, school, and district improvement plans
Professional development as an expenditure	Professional learning as an investment
Improving teacher practice	Improving teaching quality and student learning
Relying on outside experts	Tapping and building internal expertise
A single career path for teachers	Multiple options for teachers to become leaders in schools
Standardization	High standards for teaching, professional learning, and student learning

children. We want key decision makers to shift their view from professional learning as an expenditure that can be cut during lean times to a necessary investment that ensures the highest quality work force necessary to ensure success at all levels of the organization. Recasting professional development as an investment rather than an expenditure would mark the clear transition in the significant role professional learning plays in a district's vision and plan for retaining great teachers and ensuring all students achieve high levels of success. When the profession embraces the principles of diversity, planning, focus, impact, and collaboration, the momentum of success will breed previously unfound support for more.

From focusing on improving teacher practice to focusing on improving teaching quality and student learning.

Higher standards and increased accountability demand that we no longer measure the success of professional development by changes in teaching practice. Professional learning exists primarily to support educators in their commitment to serve students. As a result, we want to distinguish among different options for professional learning by their impact on educator practice as well as student learning. We believe this will lead to the development of more models for evaluating professional learning. The emphasis on evaluation will strengthen not only professional learning but also the entire education profession. When the profession embraces the principles of planning, impact, and teacher expertise, improved student learning will be the result of effective professional learning.

From a reliance on outside experts to tapping and building internal expertise.

NSDC has long held the view that the expertise to improve schools resides within the experts who work in schools. Soon, educators will recognize that the keys to unlocking the challenge of helping all students to achieve success rests on the ability to tap the expertise of each individual in school. Presented with challenges identified by data, teachers will become accustomed to looking for solutions from their colleagues in their school or in their system. Professional learning teams will offer safe space for rich and productive conversations on how to ensure the success of all students. New teachers will regularly seek the advice and support of more experienced teachers. And experienced teachers will view it as a responsibility to enable new teachers to achieve early success. Experienced teachers will be challenged to improve and turn to their colleagues for support and opportunity to learn. When the profession embraces the principles of diversity, teacher expertise, and collaboration, all schools will understand the power they have to improve themselves daily.

From a focus on a single career path for

teachers to multiple options for teachers to become leaders in their schools.

In the 20th century, teachers seeking advancement chose between counselor, principal, or consultant. Teachers in the 21st century will choose from mentor, master, instructional coach, and school-based staff developer. Schools will recognize the benefit of providing differentiated leadership opportunities for teachers, additional training and support for grade-level and department chairs so that they can provide the leadership and support that will advance teacher performance and student learning. School-based staff developers, teacher leaders, and/or coaches with a deep understanding of the day-to-day work of educators in schools will offer on-the-job assistance immediately as needed. With these options available, the problem of great teachers seeking leadership opportunities beyond the school may dissipate. More principals and superintendents will turn to teacher leaders when particular problems are identified in schools. Teachers will experience renewed respect and support from the public and hopefully teachers will be compensated for additional responsibilities and new roles. When the profession commits to the principles of diversity, leadership, and teacher expertise, more outstanding teachers will make teacher leadership a career goal.

From a focus on standardization to a focus on high standards for teaching, professional learning, and student learning.

A frequent criticism of the standards and accountability movement is that schools would lower standards for students rather than increase expectations. While standardization may point to one level of expectation, schools must ensure that every student experiences great teaching every day. This does not mean standardizing every experience but instead it requires consistent high expectations for all staff members and students. This will be achieved when educators embrace high expectations for learning for all students and high expectations for themselves from their colleagues. When the profession commits to diversity, leadership, planning, focus, impact, teacher expertise, and collaboration, all students will achieve high standards of success.

When students experience great teaching, the magic of learning explodes. However, sometimes other students in the same school and at the same grade level do not share the same joyful and productive learning experiences. If public education is to fulfill its promise that every student achieves high standards, then we can no longer allow some students to experience less than others. With the extensive research available about student learning, the widespread demand for results, technology to ease and facilitate communication and information access, rigorous curricula, and adequate instructional materials, we can prevent inequitable education in every school. We can ensure that every student's education is enriched with the extensive expertise and best thinking of all educators within the school, grade, team, or department. Our primary approach is collaborative professional learning, embedded into teachers' workday, in which all teachers learn with and from each other to ensure the highest quality teaching to every student.

Professional learning is no longer an individual experience or choice, but rather the responsibility of professional educators who are committed to both their own success and that of their colleagues. The professional learning that makes a difference and benefits all, not just some, students:

- Uses principles to establish a common set of beliefs to guide actions;
- Ensures diversity, in all its manifestations, to produce higher-quality decisions;
- Shares leadership and focus on instruction to increase results;
- Begins with bold goals and ambitious plans;
- Focuses on improving teaching and learning;
- Uses evaluation to assess results and improve practice;
- Builds on the expertise within a school and its community; and
- Creates systems to support collaboration in role-alike, grade-level, course or subject, and schoolwide learning teams to improve performance of all educators and students.

In the last decade, we have made tremendous progress in improving the effectiveness of professional learning, yet the distance to travel to achieve the vision is substantial. But we are confident that countless educators and community stakeholders are ready to redouble their efforts to make effective professional learning a part of every educator's workday so every student achieves.

About the authors

Stephanie Hirsh is executive director of the National Staff Development Council.

She joined NSDC as associate executive director in 1988, became deputy executive director in 2000, and executive director in 2007. Since joining the organization, she has played a significant role in developing the Council's conferences, affiliates, and in developing the Council's state and federal policy and advocacy agenda. In recent years, she has been NSDC's primary liaison with numerous national organizations and foundations, including Microsoft, the U.S. Department of Education, the National Education Association, the National Forum to Accelerate Middle Grades Reform, Measured Progress, National High School Alliance, American Federation of Teachers, The Wachovia Foundation, Texas Instruments, Bill and Melinda Gates Foundation, and Geraldine R. Dodge Foundation.

Hirsh facilitated the process that led to the initial set of NSDC's Standards for Staff Development as well as their revision in 2001. She later led the development of a set of innovation configurations and a Standards Assessment Inventory to support and extend that work. She is co-author of six books — co-author with Shirley Hord and Patricia Roy, *Moving NSDC's Staff Development Standards into Practice, Volume II* (NSDC, 2005); co-author with Kay Psencik, *Transforming Schools through Powerful Planning* (NSDC, 2004); co-author with Dennis Sparks, *New Vision for Staff Development* (ASCD & NSDC, 1997); co-author with Ann Delehant and Sherry Sparks, *Keys to Successful Meetings* (NSDC, 1994); co-author with Mike Murphy, *School Improvement Planning Manual* (NSDC, 1991); and co-author with Gerald Ponder and Karen Wiggins, *Exploring Texas* (Steck Vaughn, 1985).

Hirsh has a Ph.D. in curriculum and instruction from the University of North Texas.

She began her career as a classroom teacher in the Richardson (Texas) Independent School District, later becoming director of program and staff development for the district. She also served three terms on the Richardson Board of Trustees. She lives in Dallas, Texas.

Joellen Killion is deputy executive director of the National Staff Development Council. She joined NSDC in 1999 as director of special projects. She is director of NSDC's highly acclaimed NSDC Academy for Staff Developers and also has managed numerous projects for the Council, including its programs for Results-Based Staff Development, Assessing the Impact of Staff Development, Results Skills for School Leaders, School-Based Staff Developers, and NSDC's Coaches Academy. She has significant expertise in results-driven staff development, evaluation of staff development, and online professional development.

Killion is co-author with Cindy Harrison of *Taking the Lead: New Roles for Teachers and School-based Coaches* (NSDC, 2006). She is author of *Assessing Impact: Evaluating Staff Development*, 2nd ed. (Corwin & NSDC, 2007) and NSDC's three-volume results-based staff development series, *What Works in the Middle: Results-Based Staff Development* (1999), *What Works in the Elementary Grades: Results-Based Staff Development* (2001), and *What Works in the High School: Results-Based Staff Development* (2001), which summarizes studies of content-specific staff development for various grade levels. She also authored *E-learning for Educators: Implementing the Standards for Staff Development* (NSDC & NICI, 2001).

Her book, *Collaborative Professional Learning at School and Beyond: A Tool Kit for New Jersey Educators*, published in partnership with the New Jersey Department of Education in 2006, is being used by schools throughout that state to support the implementation of school-based staff development.

Killion is a former school district staff developer, curriculum coordinator, and teacher in the Adams 12 Five Star School District in suburban Denver, Colo. She was a member of the National Staff Development Council Board of Trustees and served a term as president of the organization. She lives in suburban Denver.